Fami_____e
READING FUN

Help children become successful listeners, speakers, thinkers, readers and writers

A Resource for
Parents, Teachers & Tutors

FIFTH EDITION

Kendall Hunt
publishing company

LINDA CLINARD

Author Information for Correspondence and Workshops
Linda Clinard
E-mail: Lclinard@uci.edu

English version: Hard Copy & Digital eBook
www.kendallhunt.com/clinard

Spanish Extracts: Hard Copy & Digital eBook
https://he.kendallhunt.com/product/family-time-reading-fun-spanish-extracts

Cover images © Shutterstock.com

www.kendallhunt.com
Send all inquiries to:
4050 Westmark Drive
Dubuque, IA 52004-1840

Dedication

To my newest teachers: Our grandchildren ...
- Jeff & Jamie's Madelyn & Coen
- Trevor & Holly's Hazel, Dashiell, & Hannah
- Anne & Tim's Russell

A SPECIAL "THANK YOU" TO MY NEWEST TEACHERS!

Anne, Jeff, and Trevor were my best literacy "teachers" as they were growing up and are still teaching me so much as parents of our six wonderful grandchildren. Through them I learned so much that confirmed what research and my professional experiences had prompted me to believe about how young children develop literacy. We had fun putting everyday literacy experiences into action as they showed me how they listen, speak, think, read, and write from the time they were very young.

We are so grateful for our six grandchildren who are having so much literacy fun thanks to their supportive parents. All are under 7 years old, and I continue to learn so much from them: Jeff & Jamie's Madelyn and Coen; Trevor & Holly's Hazel, Dashiell, and Hannah; and Anne & Tim's Russell.

© Jamie Clinard

Maddie and Coen enjoy bedtime.

© Anne Watson

Russell reads to his dog, Henry.

© Holly Clinard

Hazel reads to baby sister, Hannah.

© Trevor Clinard

Dashiell and Hazel read at bedtime.

Contents

About the Author   vii

Introduction   ix

    GOALS   ix

    AUDIENCE   ix

    WHO WILL BENEFIT?   ix

    HOW IS THIS BOOK ORGANIZED?   x

PART 1 Ten Keys to Literacy   1

PART 2 Influences on Literacy Development   7

    Attitude and Interests   8

    Physical Factors   9

    Expectations   14

    Everyday Literacy Experiences and Resources   16

    Tests and Other Assessments   18

PART 3 Literacy Strategies: Activities with a Purpose   25

Reading: Foundational Skills   27

    ABC Book   30

    Alpha   33

    Breaking Up Is Hard to Do   35

    Clapping Machines   36

    Do You Hear an Echo?   37

    Drivin' to the Beat   38

    Finger Walk   39

    Fun on Board   40

    Green Means Go   41

    In the Bag   42

    Is It Too Hard?   43

    Joking Around   44

    Land on It!   45

    Leave It Out   47

    Letter Art   48

    Make a Game of It   49

    Make a Match   50

    More Fun Than One   51

    Mystery Word   52

    Record It   53

    Seeing and Saying Key Words   54

    Seeing How We Read and Write Sentences   56

    Shop 'Til You Drop   57

    Shopping for Words   58

    Shout It and Write It—I'm So Proud!   59

    Silly Sounds   60

    Tap Dancer   61

    Trace-Over Art   62

    What a Character!   63

    Wonderful Words   64

    Word Speed-Up   65

Speaking and Listening   68

    Ask More and Tell Less   70

    Career Field Trip   71

    Check, Please!   72

    Child Chat   73

    Draw a Word   74

    Going to the Doctor   76

    Hear It First   77

    Hide and Guess   79

    Lights, Camera, Action!   80

    News Reporter   81

    Parent/Student/Teacher Meeting   82

    Play-by-Play   84

    Question and Answer Time   85

    Say It Like You Mean It   86

    Take Charge   87

    Tell Me More   89

Language   91

    At Close Range   93

    Call It as You See It   94

    Charted Letters   95

    Cleaning Day Fun   97

    Computer Fun with New Words   98

    Demonstration Station   99

    Down to a System   100

    Far, Far Away   101

    Feeling Good!   102

Not-a-Bore Chore   103
Personal Speller   104
Picture What You Mean!   105
Rainbow Word Trace-Over   107
Sentence Scramble   108
Shake It. Make It.   109
Story Words   110
Taking Turns   111
The Right Fit   112
Thematic Picture Dictionary   113
Wish Lists   115

Reading: Literature and Informational Text   116
Before, During, and After   118
Go and Know   119
I Can Read It and Do It   122
It's Fun to Organize   123
Laugh It Up   126
Picture It   127
Positive Role Models   128
Reading All Around   129
Reading Is Everywhere!   130
Show It When You Know It   131
Stump the Grown-Up   132
Take a Wild Guess   133

Writing   134
A Special Place   136
Be on the Lookout   137
Break It Up   138
Create a Caption   139
Gifts for Writing Fun!   140
Good-Work Meeting Day   141

Less May Be Best   142
Letter-Message Guide   144
My Daily Schedule   145
No Boundaries   146
Notice the "Good Stuff"   147
Perfect Pen Pals   148
Playing Secretary   149
See Writing Grow   150
Sloppy Copy   152
The Writing Process   153
To-Do Lists   154
Turn It Around   155
Why Read and Write?   156
Write Away   158
"Write On"   159

Appendix A: References and Family Literacy Resources   160

Appendix B: Online Resources for Parents and Teachers   162
Online Family Literacy Resources   162
Online Children's Book Lists   164
Online Dictionaries for Parents, Teachers, and Students   164

Appendix C: Introduction to National K-5 Common Core State Standards   165
Common Core Standards for English Language Arts & Literacy in History/Social Studies, Science, and Technical Subjects   167

Appendix D: Strategies and Goals   168

About the Author

Linda McCorkel Clinard earned her Ph.D. from The University of Michigan with a focus on curriculum development and teacher education, her M.S. degree in reading education from Indiana University, and her B.A. in K-8 Education from Biola University, La Mirada, California. She received the California Reading Association Margaret Lynch Community Service Award in 2003, the Orange County (California) Reading Association "Outstanding Contribution to Reading Award" in 2001, and the Michigan "International Reading Association Literacy Award" in 1988. Linda was honored to receive a Lifetime Achievement Award in 2014 from Biola University.

© Anne Watson

Dr. Clinard has served as an elementary and secondary classroom teacher and reading specialist in California, Illinois, Michigan, New York, and overseas for the Department of Defense Schools in Babenhausen, Germany and Okinawa, Japan. Dr. Clinard taught reading/literacy education courses for Michigan State University, The University of Michigan, and the University of California-Irvine School of Education. She retired from UCI in 2007 after teaching reading education for twelve years in the UCI School of Education and serving for seven years as site director of the California Reading and Literature Project in the UCI Center for Educational Partnerships. As CRLP Director, she facilitated professional development for PreK-Grade 12 partners with a goal of developing literacy leaders and improving reading, writing, and other literacy skills for all students.

Dr. Clinard currently serves as an early literacy consultant and delivers presentations for schools and the community that focus on important literacy information for families and fun everyday literacy activities that support learning at home, at school, and beyond. She volunteers at Pretend City Children's Museum, where she hosts the Literacy Carpet for the Baby Steps events (0-18 months) twice a month. For her contributions to the community, Pretend City nominated

Linda to receive a 2020 Orange County Spirit of Volunteerism Award.

She wrote *Family Time Reading Fun* to share with families and educators experience-based and research-supported information and fun activities that will help children grow as listeners, speakers, thinkers, readers, and writers. She is grateful to share information and activities that come from her wide range of personal and professional experiences as a parent (a daughter and twin sons), grandmother (three girls and three boys), classroom teacher, reading specialist, university lecturer, researcher, and professional development leader.

© *Virginia Toppert*

Photo: Linda-age 2
Jualita (Grandmother)-Salome Dominguez
Father-Harry McCorkel
Mother – Helen Dominguez McCorkel

Linda also brings insights gained from her mother who immigrated to the United States from Mexico at age eight to face the challenges of learning English. Her grandmother, whom she called "Jualita," lived with her family in Chicago, Illinois, until Jualita passed away when Linda was twelve. Linda's grandmother spoke only Spanish, so Linda spoke Spanish until age 12. After her grandmother passed away, Linda was told she didn't need to speak Spanish any longer. Her parents said, "We are in America and need to speak English. Jualita can understand any language now that she is in heaven." When Linda speaks with families whose first language is not English, she encourages the families to give their children the gift of speaking their first language fluently, as she has found that this enhances their ability to learn English.

Introduction

Parents and other family members want to help children become better readers, writers, all-around students, and productive citizens of the future.

Parents, grandparents, teachers, tutors, after-school providers, and others who support children's learning want to guide children to use activities that will develop literacy at home and in a child's everyday life, while they guide children to meet state and national learning standards and expectations.

GOALS

Family Time Reading Fun is designed as a resource for parents, teachers, literacy tutors, and after-school providers to:

- Work together to improve literacy (listening, speaking, thinking, reading, and writing) at home, school, and beyond.

- Apply *fun*, authentic, real-life literacy strategies that will connect with students' classroom instructional materials and grade-level expectations.

- Use research-supported strategies in fun, meaningful ways.

- Address grade-level expectations and high standards of performance in the context of real-world, authentic situations.

- Select appropriate, purposeful strategies that build upon students' literacy strengths and improve areas of greatest need.

AUDIENCE

This book is written to parents/caregivers, teachers, after-school providers, and tutors.

WHO WILL BENEFIT?

Information and activities will support students in grades K-5 and can be adapted for younger children. See grade levels suggested next to each activity in Part 3. Appendix D identifies standards for each activity. The expectations for each strategy are based upon the 2010 national K-5 *Common Core State Standards for English Language Arts & Literacy in History/Social Studies.* The K-5 *Common Core State Standards* are introduced in Appendix C.

© Jamie Clinard

When families of all backgrounds are engaged in their children's learning, their children tend to do better in school, stay in school longer, and pursue higher education. Clearly, children at risk of failure or poor performance can profit from the extra support that engaged families and community provide.

Henderson, A. T., Mapp, K. L., 2002, p. 73

Children's experiences before they enter school matter—research shows that children who experience high-quality care and education, and who enter school well prepared, are more successful in school and later in their lives.

North Carolina Foundations for Early Learning and Development © 2013. North Carolina Foundations Task Force. Pg. 1 (https://ncchildcare.ncdhhs. gov/Portals/0/documents/pdf/N/ NC_Foundations.pdf)

All children will benefit …

- Strong and struggling listeners, speakers, readers, and writers.
- Children for whom English is a second language.

HOW IS THIS BOOK ORGANIZED?

Part 1: Ten Keys to Literacy

The Ten Keys to Literacy highlight concepts that provide a foundation for the information and activities shared throughout *Family Time Reading Fun*. Each of the ten keys is supported by the author's 50+ years as an educator and over 40 years of exploring and participating in family literacy research and practice.

Part 2: Influences on Literacy Development

Part 2 introduces six major influences on a child's overall literacy development. One goal for Part 2 is to address the question: *Why do children with similar experiences at home and school learn to read and write and develop other literacy skills so differently?*

Part 3: Literacy Strategies: Activities with a Purpose

Part 3 introduces everyday, fun literacy strategies that are most effective in helping children grow as listeners, speakers, thinkers, readers, and writers. Each strategy is linked to kindergarten-through-grade-five expectations. See Appendices C and D for details.

There are a number of excellent reviews of literature which show that virtually all students require some explicit and systematic instruction in the alphabetic principle and phonics to learn to read and that some children require greater amounts than others.

Connor, 2011; Foorman and Connor, 2010; MacArthur, et. al, 2001; Reis, McCoach, Little, Muller, & Kaniskan, 2011; Stuebing, et. al., 2008; Weiser & Mathes, 2011

Connor, C. Ed. (2016) *The Cognitive Development of Reading and Reading Comprehension.* Routledge. New York, p. 171

Part 3 offers over 100 everyday literacy strategies in five categories aligned with the K-5 *Common Core State Standards for English Language Arts & Literacy in History/Social Studies, Science, and Technical Subjects* (http://www.corestandards.org/ELA-Literacy/)

The K-5 standards define what students should understand and be able to do by the end of each grade. Standards within each of the five Common Core State Standards (CCSS) categories are identified within specific literacy skills listed under each of the five categories below.

1. Literacy-Reading: Foundational Skills

   - Print Concepts (K-1)

   - Phonological Awareness (K-1)

   - Phonics and Word Recognition (K-5)

   - Fluency (K-5)

2. Speaking and Listening
   - Comprehension and Collaboration
   - Presentation of Knowledge and Ideas
3. Language
   - Conventions of Standard English
   - Knowledge of Language (Begins at Grade 2)
4. Reading: Literature and Informational Text
   - Key Ideas and Details
   - Craft and Structure
   - Integration of Knowledge and Ideas
   - Range of Reading and Level of Text Complexity
5. Writing
   - Text Types and Purposes
   - Production and Distribution of Writing
   - Research to Build and Present Knowledge
   - Range of Writing (Begins at Grade 2)

Each strategy in Appendix D is linked to K-5 expectations, as applicable, selected from the *Common Core State Standards for English Language Arts & Literacy in History/Social Studies, Science, and Technical Subjects.*

Appendix A: References and Family Literacy Resources

Appendix A lists references and resources to support family literacy. References are listed for quotes and other resources cited throughout the book.

Appendix B: Online Resources for Parents and Teachers

Online resources for parents and teachers are listed in three categories: (1) *Online Family Literacy Resources*; (2) *Online Children's Book List*; (3) *Online Dictionaries for Parents, Teachers, and Students.*

Appendix C: Introduction to National K-5 Common Core State Standards

Appendix C provides an introduction to the Common Core State Standards for English Language Arts & Literacy in History/Social Studies, Science, and Technical Subjects

Appendix D: Strategies and Standards

Each strategy in Part 3 is linked to appropriate Common Core State Standards for English Language Arts & Literacy in History/Social Studies, Science, and Technical Subjects.

Common Core State Standards for English Language Arts & The Literacy in History/Social Studies, Science, and Technical Subjects ("the standards") represent the next generation of K–12 standards designed to prepare all students for success in college, career, and life by the time they graduate from high school.

The standards establish guidelines for English language arts (ELA) as well as for literacy in history/social studies, science, and technical subjects. Because students must learn to read, write, speak, listen, and use language effectively in a variety of content areas, the standards promote the literacy skills and concepts required for college and career readiness in multiple disciplines.

http://www.corestandards.org/ELA-Literacy/

Ten Keys to Literacy

The Ten Keys to Literacy are important concepts to keep in mind as you guide a child to become a proficient reader and writer. These "ten keys to literacy" are part of everyday experiences, and their importance is confirmed in professional literature and reflected by effective teaching practices.

TEN KEYS TO LITERACY

1. Literacy is more than knowing how to read and write.

2. Everyone has literacy strengths.

3. The Alphabetic Principle provides an important foundation for helping to "crack the code" of written language by learning essential skills such as letter-sounds and phonics.

4. Literacy requires us to become involved and use words for many purposes, in all subject areas, and in many ways as part of our everyday lives. Involvement helps us become literate.

5. Progress in literacy cannot be measured by test scores and grades alone.

6. Children develop literacy at different rates and in different ways.

7. Literacy is a process that begins in the early years. It is not instant.

8. Specific goals are needed to help children succeed as listeners, speakers, readers, and writers.

9. Personal information, background knowledge, resources, and making choices to support motivation are factors that influence literacy development.

10. Parents, grandparents, teachers, tutors, and others who are helping children develop literacy should offer practical guidance, avoid applying pressure, and HAVE FUN!

Early language and literacy skills are learned best through everyday moments with your child—reading books, talking, laughing, and playing together. Children learn language when you talk to them and they communicate back to you, and by hearing stories read and songs sung aloud.
Zero to Three-*Supporting Language and Literacy Skills from 0-12 months* (2010).

© Jamie Clinard

The following information and research-related quotes offer more detail about the *Ten Keys to Literacy*. Parents and others are encouraged to remember these Keys as they support children in growing as listeners, speakers, thinkers, readers, and writers.

1. **Literacy is more than knowing how to read and write.** When we are literate, we use listening, speaking, thinking, reading, and writing to communicate wants, needs, feelings, and ideas and to solve problems and complete tasks. Literacy applies to many areas of life, and can be as natural as listening to a phone message and texting a reply. We can be literate in everyday languages from different cultures that use a wide variety of spoken and written forms of communication.

There are four types of vocabulary: listening, speaking, reading, and writing. Each type has a different purpose; fortunately vocabulary development in one type facilitates growth in another.
Montgomery, J. (2019) p. 2

2. **Everyone has literacy strengths.** We all differ in how and why we listen, speak, think, read, and write, but each of us has strengths in one or more of these areas! We tend to try harder when we are aware of what we do well. Whether you are a parent, learner, or teacher, you should *stress a strength and nurture a need.* Ideally, we should build on a child's literacy accomplishments as we respectfully nurture the child's needs. When you focus on telling children what they are doing right, and offer help and guidance in areas that need support, they often try harder to do things independently, and ask for help as needed. For example, we told our son we were proud that he followed the directions in the Cub Scout manual to learn how to tie various knots on his own. He asked for our help when he was invited to speak to the Cub Scouts about how he had followed directions for different knots without help from others.

Monitoring progress is at the heart of a successful program in which instruction is differentiated. Teachers who respect and respond to variability are constantly alert to individual needs and the implications for instruction. They use assessment to focus on students' strengths rather than just their weaknesses.
Strickland, D. S., Ganske, K, & Monroe, J. K. (2002), Pg. 50

© Linda Clinard

3. **The Alphabetic Principle provides an important foundation for helping to "crack the code" of written language by learning essential skills such as letter-sounds and phonics.** For many years literacy researchers have strongly stressed the importance of the Alphabetic Principle, understanding that letters represent sounds of language (phonemes) and these letters and sounds blend together to make words. Dr. Connie Juel, a Stanford University distinguished retired professor, wrote, *"Letter-sound knowledge is prerequisite to effective word identification. A primary difference between good and poor readers is the ability to use letter-sound correspondence to identify words"* (Juel, 1991). Keith Stanovich, another highly-respected retired professor and literacy researcher from the

Children need careful and highly technical instruction if they are to learn to read and write well (Adams, 1990). First, they must master the alphabetic principle— that letters stand for sounds and that the letters combine to create words that have meaning. Then, they have to learn how to make sense of what they have decoded, which is even more difficult. . . . English is among the most difficult languages to read and write: the spelling is irregular and the vocabulary is vast.
Connor, C. -Ed. (2016), p. 1

University of Toronto wrote, "*Students who acquire and apply the alphabetic principle early in their reading careers reap long-term benefits.*"

4. **Literacy requires us to become involved and use words for many purposes, in all subject areas, and in many ways as part of our everyday lives. Involvement helps us become literate.**
Our son and his daughter have enjoyed "Science Saturdays" since she was three years old, enjoying everyday, fun science experiments. These weekly experiments are a great example of how children can be involved when …

© Trevor Clinard

- there is interaction with others in meaningful, fun everyday experiences.

- you work toward goals diligently, and literacy is applied in all areas of study—physical science, mathematics, social science, the arts … and more.

- the senses of hearing, seeing, tasting, touching, and smelling are used to gather and communicate information.

Subject-specific terminology can help learners at all age levels grow as they better understand the subject and communicate what they are learning. They also grow as they become proficient in using language related to areas of their interest, such as terms used in online games, sports, and hobbies.

5. **Progress in literacy cannot be measured by test scores and grades alone.** Checklists, report cards, and test scores can be helpful indicators of where children are in the process of becoming literate, but they should not be accepted as the only indicators. Literacy should also be measured by observing, recording, and keeping samples of how thinking, listening, speaking, reading, and writing are meaningfully applied in a child's daily life. Writing dates on what children write and draw helps us see growth over time. (See Part 2: *Testing Experiences* for more information.)

Reward children for growth, not for outperforming others.
Pressley (2006), p. 386

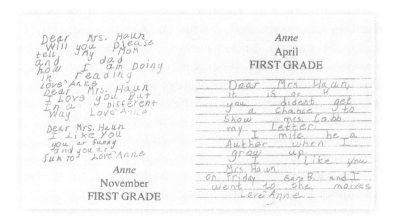

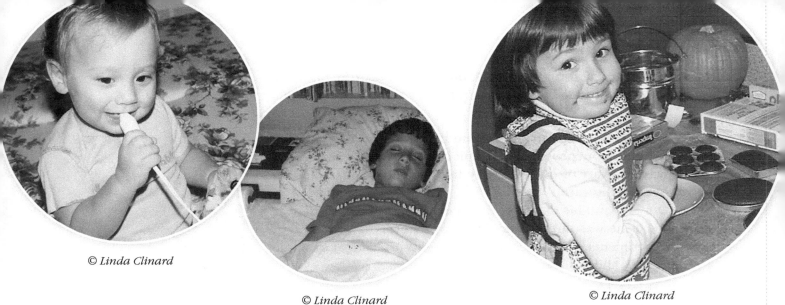

© Linda Clinard

© Linda Clinard

© Linda Clinard

6. **Children develop literacy at different rates and in different ways.** No two children are created the same, and no two learn in the same way. This fact was confirmed when our identical twin sons, Jeff and Trevor, grew up with very different interests. Jeff had fun speaking into real and pretend microphones from the time he was a toddler. Trevor enjoyed playing with adding machines and numbers from the time he was very young … even taking them to bed with him. In college, Jeff earned his bachelor's degree in Communication Studies. Trevor earned undergraduate and graduate degrees in Business and Finance. Our daughter, Anne, always showed an interest in cooking with me, and would ask me to please take a photo of what we made. Today, Anne is an award-winning food photographer. Our family has confirmed what the California State University Center for Advancement of Reading and Writing has said for many years. Children's interests and talents when they are very young are "strengths" that should be acknowledged and can influence their futures.

7. **Literacy is a process that begins in the early years. It is not instant.** The literacy process begins at infancy and grows throughout a lifetime. Literacy begins when an infant sees, hears, smells, tastes, and touches the world around them. As young children are guided to develop meaning from what they experience every day, the groundwork for literacy is being laid. The literacy process continues throughout our lives and is not instant at any stage in life. Because literacy skills develop in various ways and at various times for each individual, we should be patient and guide each child to learn at a rate that shows steady progress over time. Some may learn quickly to decode and attach meaning to what they read, while others need more time. Such differences are quite normal.

8. **Specific goals are needed to help children succeed as listeners, speakers, readers, and writers.** Parents and teachers often feel they struggle between what they know children need to better develop literacy, and what public pressure says is needed. To resist pressure from others, parents and teachers need to work together to focus on four goals to help children succeed.

- *Help children feel safe to try, and set learning goals with your child.* We learn best when we feel safe to take risks and can try our new ideas and learn without criticism from mistakes. To help children feel safe, give genuine praise for specific accomplishments (even small ones). Set a few specific goals *with the child* to (1) build on the child's strengths, and (2) address (in a nurturing way) significant needs that are appropriate to the child's age.

- *Help children take responsibility for their own learning.* We help children develop responsibility for their learning when we create a safe environment (such as a quiet place to study), provide opportunities to explore (such as neighborhood nature walks), and ask questions that prompt thinking (such as *Why do you think the recipe did not work?*).

- *Help children be everyday learners.* Children learn from everyday experiences. We need to encourage and guide them to use literacy in everyday life. Everyday experiences include such things as reading together, gardening together, and participating in developmentally appropriate strategies selected from Part 3.

- *Help children develop a purpose for learning.* We need to guide children to see the importance of activities that involve thinking, speaking, listening, reading, and writing. One easy way to demonstrate a purpose for an activity is to simply explain how a literacy activity in which your child is engaged will help in the future with school, the family, or everyday tasks. And, the excitement of learning something new about a subject your child is interested in is a great motivation.

9. **Personal information, background knowledge, resources, and making choices to support motivation are factors that influence literacy development.** See Part 2 of *Family Time Reading Fun* for other detailed influences on literacy development. As you select activities to support a child's literacy learning, ask, *How do the following factors and others in Part 2 impact the child's literacy development?*

- **Personal information** A child's age, grade, interests, attitude, eyesight, hearing, general health, educational experiences, and more are factors that influence literacy development.

- **Background knowledge** Children bring a wide range of background knowledge to their listening, thinking, reading, and writing experiences at home and beyond. Knowing a child's background can be ideal for *stressing a strength*.

. . . early experience with language, beginning in infancy, promotes fluency in understanding and growth in vocabulary, building a foundation for later literacy.
Neumann and Dickinson (2011), p. 3

Developmentally appropriate practice does not mean making things easier for children. Rather, it means ensuring that goals and experiences are suited to their learning and development AND challenging enough to promote their progress and interest.
Copple and Bredekamp, 2009, p. xii

. . . effective classrooms always include the following messages:

1. *Trying hard fosters achievement and intelligence.*
2. *Failure is a natural part of learning.*
3. *Being best is not what school is about; getting better is.*

Pressley (2006), p. 379

It is clear from the research that the process of learning to read is a lengthy one that begins very early in life. ***Given the importance identified in the research literature of starting school motivated*** *to read and with* ***the prerequisite language and early literacy skills*** *. . . all children, especially those at risk for reading difficulties, should have access to early childhood environments that promote language and literacy growth . . .*
Snow, Burns, Griffin (1998), p. 8

- **Resources** How available are resources that support literacy, such as technology tools and programs, audiobooks, games, and writing materials, such as paper, pens, pencils, crayons, markers ...?

- **Making choices to support motivation** Encouraging children to choose books they would like to read from the time they are very young can increase their desire and motivation to read. Researchers have found that allowing students to make choices about their reading material increases the likelihood that they will engage more in reading (Worthy and McKool, 1996), and other studies suggest that providing genuine student choices increases effort and commitment to reading (Guthrie and Wigfield, 2000). Our grandson has always loved to choose books about vehicles from the time he was very young. Today he is motivated to read so much more.

© Anne Watson

10. **Parents, grandparents, teachers, tutors, and others who are helping children develop literacy should offer practical guidance, avoid applying pressure, and HAVE FUN!** We need to offer practical literacy experiences that fit meaningfully into children's daily lives, so children can be happy while learning at the same time.

Instead of applying pressure, we must offer guidance. Pressure works "behind" children and pushes them along. Children are not always aware of the goal they are trying to achieve when they are pressured or pushed too hard and too fast. On the other hand, children who are guided and praised for even small accomplishments assume more ownership and self-motivation for continually improving. Follow these effective ways to offer guidance instead of applying pressure:

- **Invite children to choose** books, activities, and materials that will support learning.

- **Acknowledge children's accomplishments** by telling them what you see them doing well.

- **Ask questions** about children's literacy experiences, listen to their responses, and engage in further conversation.

- **Guide children to self-evaluate** their literacy performance and set goals to build on their strengths while nurturing their needs.

We need to serve as a guide, model, and support as we work with children to apply the "Ten Keys to Literacy" at home, at school, and beyond ... into the real world.

Influences on Literacy Development

Parents and teachers have told me they welcome learning about significant areas that can influence literacy development, regardless of a child's age or background ... especially when I use examples of how our identical twin sons grew up with very different interests and challenges. Both are successful businessmen today. Four factors that influence learning were introduced in Part 1. They include *personal information, background knowledge, resources,* and *making choices to support motivation.* Part 2 offers further details about areas that influence literacy development for children of all ages.

INFLUENCES ON LITERACY DEVELOPMENT

ATTITUDE AND INTERESTS	How does a child respond when faced with opportunities to speak, listen, read, and write in daily life?
PHYSICAL FACTORS	Are vision, hearing, eating habits, sleeping habits, or other physical factors helping or hindering a child's literacy growth?
EXPECTATIONS	How do adults' expectations and actions influence a child's literacy development?
EVERYDAY LITERACY EXPERIENCES AND RESOURCES	Does the child have access to a variety of everyday experiences and resources that enhance literacy development?
TESTS AND OTHER ASSESSMENTS	Are parents, teachers, and students using assessment information in the most effective way to support literacy progress?
PARENTS!	Parents influence their child's learning experiences and literacy development in many ways.

Anyone who has ever observed how different children from the same family behave knows that all children do not learn, respond, and think in the same manner. Successful parents recognize the differences in their children, adjust their routines, and interact accordingly, in order to maximize the potential of each of their children.
Cunningham and Allington (2011)

Families and communities are vital partners in fostering young children's literacy development. The special ways that babies and their family communicate, based upon trust, familiarity, and family routines, form what some researchers call their "roots of literacy".
California State University Center for Advancement of Reading and Writing (2019) p. 4

Parents (whether biological parents, adoptive parents, or other primary caregivers) play an essential role in the cognitive development, including language and literacy development, through the learning environments they provide for children.
Connor, C.-Ed. (2016) p. 120

Attitude and Interests

• Listening

• Speaking

• Thinking

• Reading

• Writing

...intervention results suggest that culturally sensitive teaching that includes motivation materials and individualized instruction should promote literacy skills across ethnicities ... Motivation is a key component to maximize successful outcomes.
Connor, C.- Ed. (2016) p. 145

Many factors contribute to children's motivation in learning to read and write—their interest, attitude, and engagement. Findings from recent research suggest that not only does motivation to read have many dimensions. but also different students are motivated in different ways ...
Strickland, Ganske, & Monroe (2002) p. 16, 22

Do not tuch you do you in deep trubel

© Linda Clinard

Attitude and Interests

A child's attitude and level of interest greatly influence motivation to learn and become literate.

Consider how attitudes and interests influence the following literacy skills.

Listening Encourage your child to listen to familiar and new ideas while you enjoy a discussion about what has been heard. Do not remain silent when your child does not seem interested. Talk with your child and encourage participation in the discussion.

Speaking Children naturally want to talk about their interests. Continue those discussions and enhance them by asking open-ended questions. As a child speaks more frequently, confidence will be gained and a positive attitude about speaking will develop. Oral language provides a strong foundation for reading and writing.

Thinking As children develop an interest in things around their home and in the world, we can help them think about how their interests at home can be linked to what they are learning and experiencing at school. As your child thinks about how what they enjoy doing outside of school can be linked to what they learn in school, they are more likely to take risks and responsibility for learning that will support them in the future.

Reading Attitude and interest make a difference in how much a child chooses to read independently. Surround children with reading materials that interest them, even if it is reading materials you do not find interesting. Be an example. Children should see adults read daily, whether they are reading a magazine, map, recipe, online information, or a book—either hard copy or eBook.

Writing Writing is communicating in a printed form for a wide range of purposes. Some writing experiences follow a process that includes writing a draft and other steps that lead to a final version after spelling and punctuation have been checked and complete, clear thoughts are expressed. Most writing, however, may be meaningful "first-draft" experiences such as journals, email, phone messages, letters/notes to relatives/friends, or a child's note such as the one our son put on his favorite toy when he was 6 years old. Children need frequent, meaningful writing experiences that include first-draft-only experience *and* other experiences that follow a writing process from early drafts to final copy.

Physical Factors

There are a number of physical factors that influence a child's literacy development. A child's fine and gross motor skills can affect literacy-related experiences. Also, vision and hearing are closely related to literacy performance. Eating and sleeping habits and other health-related experiences can influence a child's learning as well.

Fine Motor Skills

Fine motor skills require learners of all ages, including adults, to use the small muscles in our hands, wrists, fingers, feet, and toes. Fine motor skills are used when we …

- Write
- Hold crayons with fingers, not the fist
- Button clothing
- Turn pages
- Cut with scissors
- Send text messages on our phones
- Use keyboards on computers
- String beads

Gross Motor Skills

Gross motor skills usually involve whole-body movements which use large muscles, such as those in our arms, legs, and torso. Gross motor skills using our large muscles are needed when we …

- Run
- Jump
- Swim
- Dance
- Walk
- Stand … and *more!*

Whenever the emphasis on grades is high enough that students can convince themselves that they are reading only to obtain a high grade or other tangible reward, there is danger of undermining whatever intrinsic motivation a student might have.
Pressley (2006) p. 385

Physical Factors

- Fine Motor Skills
- Gross Motor Skills
- Vision
- Hearing
- Eating and Sleeping Habits
- Other Health-Related Issues

There are relationships between fine motor and hand-eye coordination in kindergarten and early school achievement in mathematics and language (Son and Meisel 2006). Children who fail to establish good perceptual–motor skills in preschool will not only have trouble with movement and coordination, but may also be at risk of academic failure.
California Preschool Learning Foundations, Vol. 2 (2010) p. 59

Many educators have used the *Early Childhood Environmental Rating Scale* (ECERS) developed by researchers at the University of North Carolina in 1980 to assess preschool children. Updated versions of ECERS have been written (Harms, Clifford, and Cryer 2005), and other assessments have been developed to assess infants & toddlers and school-age children ages 5–12. (https://ers.fpg.unc.edu/environment-rating-scales) The ECERS contain 35 items early childhood educators are trained to assess in natural environments in the classroom and beyond. ECERS items include gross motor skills and other observation areas related to gross and fine motor skills.

Authors of the ECERS indicate that children in full-day early childhood programs (more than four hours per day) should get one hour a day of gross motor play, and children in half-day programs should get 30 minutes (California Preschool Learning Foundations, Vol. 2, p. 40).

Vision

Seeing clearly can influence a child's literacy success. If a child is having difficulty seeing something clearly, he or she is less likely to read or write well.

We might think a child is being stubborn by refusing to complete an assignment or answer a question that requires good vision. Such reluctance may be a sign of a vision problem. If you suspect a child's eyes are contributing to frustration in learning to read and write, teachers and parents should discuss the advisability of a thorough visual examination.

Our 6-year-old granddaughter was having challenges with reading and writing in Kindergarten and at the beginning of first grade—until her parents had her eyes tested. She became immediately more comfortable when reading and writing after getting her new glasses, and she has shown steady improvement as a reader and writer.

What patterns of behavior do you see as your child reads and writes? Consider the following to help determine whether or not a child may need a visual examination:

Does the child ...

✓ have red or watery eyes?

✓ squint or cover an eye frequently?

✓ frequently say, "I have a headache" or "My eyes itch"?

✓ often skip lines when reading?

© Jamie Clinard

Numerous clinical and research studies have shown that good visual abilities are beneficial to learning to read and to read with understanding. Children with normal eyesight (20/20) can have visual problems which affect how their eyes focus, team together, or move along a line of print when reading.
College of Optometrists in Vision Development (2008)

✓ struggle to write on or between the lines on lined paper?

✓ become very tired when reading or writing?

✓ read a little at a time and look away frequently?

Be certain to describe to the optometrist or other vision specialist the behaviors observed at home and at school as your child reads and writes. A description of behaviors provides important clues for prescribing solutions.

When glasses are prescribed, parents and teachers often hear *I can't find my glasses.* Many parents and teachers discover that even when the glasses go to school, teachers rarely see them. It is important for parents and teachers to be aware of prescribed glasses and assure the child that the glasses will make them more comfortable when they are worn.

Glasses may not ensure success in learning to read. Further guidance and ongoing visual monitoring by a vision specialist may be what is required to keep your child on the road to literacy success.

Hearing
The ability to hear can influence literacy success.

Children who have frequent ear problems (fluid buildup, infections, severe allergies) can become frustrated with literacy-related tasks. Phonemic awareness (identifying and manipulating sounds that are heard in words and sentences) can be difficult. Listening to a story and understanding what they hear can also be a challenge.

Be aware of everyday signals that provide evidence that a child's inability to hear clearly may be affecting literacy growth. Signals could include moving to stand closer to you when you are speaking, not responding to verbal questions, and talking more loudly than others in a conversation. If you suspect your child may have a hearing problem, note the behaviors. Parents and teachers should discuss the behaviors observed.

Do parents or teachers see any of the following behaviors that may show a need to have the child's hearing tested?

Does the child ...

✓ become frustrated with activities that require listening and following directions?

✓ become restless or distracted when listening to a story?

✓ have difficulty discriminating between similar-sounding words?

When children have trouble reading, parents and teachers need to investigate many possible causes. That's because reading difficulty usually stems from a combination of problems, rather than just one.

One potential problem that is sometimes overlooked is the child's vision. This may happen because the child appears to be able to see, does not complain about his or her eyes, or has passed a school vision screening.

Reading requires the integration of a number of vision skills ... And parents, teachers, or children often don't notice the symptoms of reading-related vision problems.

American Optometric Association (2020). Getting to the Root of Reading Problems https://www.aoa.org/patients-and-public/resources-for-teachers/a-look-at-reading-and-vision

Hearing impairment or deafness is another condition well documented to be associated with reading difficulty ... Chronic infections (chronic otitis media) often lead to intermittent hearing loss during the early years.
Snow, Burn, & Griffin (1998) p. 104

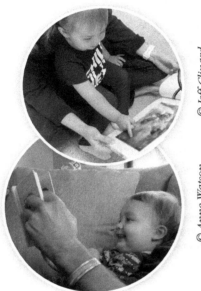

✓ know letter-sounds one moment when asked to blend sounds to read a word and forgets the letter-sounds when asked to read the word again?

✓ have frequent ear infections and/or fluid buildup?

✓ have severe allergies that cause stuffiness and/or chronic congestion?

Timing is very important when hearing is tested. It should be noted whether the hearing screenings at school or the doctor's office occur when symptoms of an allergy or infection are present. If you suspect allergies may affecting hearing, consult with a specialist to determine when a child's hearing should be tested.

We are grateful that our grandchildren do not appear to have challenges with hearing clearly. From the time when they were very young, they loved to hear their parents read to them. Today, many children enjoy audiobooks, but nothing substitutes for hearing a story while cuddling with mom and dad.

Eating and Sleeping Habits
Eating and sleeping habits influence literacy success in a variety of ways. Good eating and sleeping habits give a child energy to remain alert throughout the day. Children who get proper nutrition and enough sleep have stronger immune systems, resulting in better attention, as well as a superior attendance record at school.

Poor eating and sleeping habits can have a negative influence on literacy development. For example, some children seem to have a sensitivity to caffeine or sugar, causing a lack of concentration or trouble falling asleep at night. Others seem to become "silly" or physically more active. If you feel your child may be affected by caffeine or sugar, modify your child's diet and watch for a change in behavior.

Avoiding breakfast is another eating habit that can adversely affect school performance. Children who skip breakfast may lack energy to be attentive until lunch.

Our children taught us how children from the same family may respond very differently to what they eat and drink. When our children were young, we saw that our daughter, Anne, would have trouble falling asleep if she had any sweet treats or chocolate drinks after 3:00 or 4:00 in the afternoon. Our twin sons never demonstrated the same sensitivity.

Healthier diet assessed by the Baltic Sea Diet Score (BSDS) or the Finnish Children Healthy Eating Index (FCHEI) in Grade 1 was associated with better reading skills, but not with arithmetic skills, among children in Grades 1–3.
Haapala, E.A., Eloranta, A., Venäläinen, T. et al. (2017)

One very memorable experience was when our daughter was four years old. She was excited to play at a friend's house one afternoon and have dinner with the family before coming home around 6:30–7:00. After bringing her home, we went through the usual routines of bath time, reading a story, and playing soft music as we put her to bed around 7:30–8:00. She usually fell sound asleep within 20–30 minutes ... but not that night. We heard her talking and singing, then running around her room where there was only a night light on. We would go in every 20–30 minutes to help her go back to bed. This happened until she finally fell asleep around 11:00.

After Anne woke up at 6:30 the next morning, I asked her what she did at her friend's house the night before that may have had her too excited to fall asleep. She said, "It was so much fun having chocolate candy and chocolate ice cream for dessert and chocolate milk to drink at dinner." This experience reminded us to always remind her to tell her friends she might have trouble sleeping if she has chocolate or other sweets at dinner.

Today, Anne is an award-winning food photographer who prepares very healthy food for her family. Her six-year-old son loves to help her prepare meals. As you can see, he was very excited about the healthy foods they prepared for their family and guests.

Parents and teachers should discuss learning challenges a child may be experiencing that may be related to eating or sleeping habits. Consider introducing nutritious foods into your child's diet by preparing foods in fun ways. Make pancakes with fruit faces or sandwiches shaped with cookie cutters. For better sleep, does your child need to eat healthier foods, or have fun with more physical activities during the day?

© Anne Watson

Other Health-Related Issues

Physical and emotional health Researchers have explored how learning can be affected when children experience physical health challenges such as type 1 diabetes. Emotional/psychological health challenges such as anxiety and depression have also been studied and may influence children's learning. Dr. Carol McDonald Connor highlights and summarizes these studies in her book *The Cognitive Development of Reading and Reading Comprehension* (2016).

If you suspect that your child has a health problem, even if it does not seem to affect literacy-related tasks at school or at home, be sure to share your observations with your child's pediatrician or another health professional.

In addition to chronic psychological health issues stemming from anxiety, depression, and trauma, children's ability to be proficient in reading can also be hindered by physical health. For example, type 1 diabetes has been associated with deficits in reading and cognitive performance, although results are mixed.
Kucer & Sullivan, 2011. Connor, C. (2016) p. 115

Family literacy programs seek to enhance literacy within families ... The impetus for family-based programs is broad, ranging from (a) research on positive influence that family literacy experiences can have on subsequent literacy achievement ... (b) the relationship between parents' expectations and attitudes regarding education attainment and children's achievement ... (c) the widely held belief that it is difficult for a classroom or school to make up for the lack of literacy activities in the family.
Snow, Burns, & Griffin (1998) p. 145–146

© Jamie Clinard

Expectations

Friends, relatives, and teachers significantly influence a child's literacy development. Your response to the following questions can provide insight into how you and others can influence your child's literacy development: *What are your expectations for your child's literacy development? How do you communicate your expectations?* Expecting too much or too little affects how a child learns to read, write, or perform any task. How can we balance our expectations?

Expecting Too Much   The issue of "expecting too much" should be as much a concern as "expecting too little." Children need realistic, sensitive guidance—not pressure. Guide and support your children to take responsibility and set goals for their own success. Consider the following tips when helping children set realistic goals for themselves.

- Talk with your child to find out about skills (academic, artistic, or others) she/he wants to develop.

- Encourage your child to talk with you and the teachers about how to prioritize and list the skills that are most important.

- Help your child develop a plan for pursuing interests and developing important skills.

- Write a few short-term goals on your family calendar.

Whatever the child's age, beware of the temptation to expect too much too soon. Listen to your child for hints that goals need to be adjusted. Always be observant, thoughtful, and ready to adjust the child's schedule, goals, and plans in ways that keep the child moving forward with motivation to learn.

The importance of listening to children and helping them adjust their learning goals brings back memories from when our children were young. When Anne, Jeff, and Trevor brought home their report cards, we would meet individually with them to talk about their strengths. We also discussed "goals" to build on their strengths and other goals to address subjects or behaviors they needed to improve. Then, we would have a "family team meeting" to talk about how we could all support one another. I am so grateful that as parents today, they talk with their children when they get reports from school, and they set goals with their children.

Expecting Too Little   Some adults expect too little from children, and in turn, the children expect little of themselves. Avoid the inclination to believe that a child is not smart enough or does not have the capacity to do better. Do not let test scores or an opinion offered by a friend, relative, psychologist, or other

professional prompt you or the child to conclude that a child cannot learn or may struggle with learning. *All children can learn!* They simply learn in different ways and at different rates.

Our family learned this through a very frightening experience when our twin sons were 3 months old. The nurses who helped us on that difficult day when our son, Trevor, got very sick told us at a follow-up appointment that they called him "The boy who touched noses with God."

The boys had been eating well and very regularly until one day Trevor slept longer than usual for his morning nap. I picked him up and gently tried to wake him up to eat, but he became limp in my hands … causing me to panic and call the pediatrician and my husband, who was at work. The pediatrician said I could get to her local clinic faster than waiting for an ambulance if I left immediately. I quickly put all three children in the car. Trevor, his twin brother Jeff, and 5-year-old Anne and I rushed to the local clinic where our pediatrician was waiting. Trevor had still not awakened.

Our pediatric nurse was waiting outside the main entrance and immediately took him as we drove up. She ran into the clinic with him and told me later she had rushed ahead of me because he was turning blue and needed immediate help. As I hurried into the clinic with Anne and Jeff, I saw multiple doctors and nurses rush to the room where she took Trevor.

I waited outside the room with Anne and Jeff until our neighbor came to pick them up, and was still not permitted in the room. The doctors had advised the receptionist to call my husband John to tell him to go directly to the main Henry Ford Hospital in downtown Detroit where they planned to send us by ambulance once Trevor was stabilized. The nurse came out periodically to comfort me, but she shared no specifics.

As the nurse was talking with me about an hour after we had arrived, another nurse rushed to us and said that a pediatric anesthesiologist who was visiting the clinic from the downtown hospital did what the other pediatric nurses and doctors had not been able to do to stabilize Trevor's breathing and heart rate. She inserted a breathing tube, so Trevor could be transported downtown, and rode in the ambulance with Trevor and me. John was at the hospital when we arrived.

© Linda Clinard

Trevor was taken immediately to the Pediatric Intensive Care Unit. Soon after we arrived, the OB-GYN doctor who delivered the boys came to see us. She could tell I was exhausted and very concerned. She gave me a hug and asked to talk with me briefly outside the ICU. She said she knew I taught teachers to teach reading for Michigan State University. I was surprised to hear her ask me, "What do most educators say about children who have stopped breathing multiple times and had their heart almost stop?" I replied, "They will most likely have brain damage and severe learning disorders." Her reply shocked me: "You need to get those lies out of your mind! Trevor's brain is small and has much room to grow. You and others in your family need to treat him as you treat his brother, and believe he can learn as much as any child." The doctor's words have strongly influenced how we raised Trevor. We were so grateful that he came home from the hospital sooner than doctors originally predicted. Five-year-old Anne was so protective and supportive.

Trevor is now a wonderful husband and father of three. He is a successful businessman after earning his Bachelor of Science in Business at California Polytechnic University in San Luis Obispo and an M.B.A. graduating with honors from the University California-Irvine.

This was a long story, but I want every parent and teacher to know we can all help and support children to succeed. We need to believe they can be successful—and so do they!

© Sarah Del Pozo

Balancing Expectations
How do you balance expectations, so you do not expect too much or too little of a child? Ongoing communication among parents, teachers, and children is important. What is your child's response to everyday experiences that involve listening, speaking, thinking, reading and writing? Is your child motivated? Discouraged? Challenged? One way to balance expectations is to set realistic goals with your child based upon what you observe.

Set a good example by being positive, patient, inquisitive, self-disciplined and eager to learn new things.

Communicate regularly with those who are raising children who are happy and learning.

Everyday Literacy Experiences and Resources

Everyday Literacy Experiences and Resources

A child's everyday literacy experiences that use a variety of resources can enhance literacy development at home, at school, and beyond. Zoos, museums, and so many other places in our community offer rich resources that will support your child in developing literacy.

Everyday literacy resources can include anything that will support listening, speaking, thinking, reading, and writing. For example …

- Restaurant menus, including child-friendly menus with images such as the children's menu our grandson is reading.

- Family weekly menus—our granddaughter loves to help write her family's weekly meal plan.

- Technology in various forms that send and receive messages—our grandson asked if he could send a message on his dad's phone.

- Explore new experiences by listening as someone guides you. Our granddaughter listened carefully to her dad as he guided her to climb a rock wall.

- Invite children to help find items from the family shopping list. Our 2-year-old granddaughter chose two of her favorites from the family list by "reading" the images and logos.

Resources such libraries, museums, and child youth centers can play an important role in supporting children.
CSU Center for Advancement of Reading and Writing (2019). p. 11

© Trevor Clinard

© Jamie Clinard

© Holly Clinard

© Anne Watson

© Jamie Clinard

Tests and other Assessments

- Assessment Goals

- Look Beyond Test Scores

- Ask Questions about Tests

- Explore Different Approaches

Given that effective instruction consists of responding to children's needs while building on their strengths, it necessarily depends on a sensitive and continual capacity for monitoring student progress.
Snow, Burns, & Griffin (1998) p. 336

Much—but not all—assessment of young children can occur effectively through skilled and thoughtful observations of and interactions with children in the context of daily activities. Some assessments, particularly in cases where there is concern about the development or progress of a child, must be individually conducted by adults with specialized knowledge who use reliable and valid measures in order to obtain accurate and detailed information.
CSU Center for Advancement of Reading and Writing (2019). p. 11

Tests and Other Assessments

The knowledge that parents and teachers have about literacy tests and other assessments can have a major influence on a child's literacy performance. It is important that parents and teachers recognize that various types of literacy tests and assessments have multiple goals.

Assessment Types and Goals

The following types of literacy assessments have a wide variety of goals:

1. A "diagnostic assessment" is given to pre-assess a child's specific literacy strengths and needs for the purpose of identifying learning goals and planning meaningful support at home and school.

2. "Observational assessments" measure how well students perform related to literacy-related expectations and standards for specific grade levels.

3. Compare the literacy performance of students usually above 2nd grade with a national and/or other group norms.

Teachers are encouraged to monitor a student's literacy performance in multiple ways. For example, they may use literacy activities in class and other activities that are part of home-based assignments. They may also use information they gather from individual or group literacy tests that diagnose performance related to specific skills.

Look Beyond Test Scores

Group and individually-administered assessments, everyday literacy activities, and standards-based tests can monitor how children perform reading, writing, and other literacy tasks.

Parents and teachers are encouraged to communicate about a child's literacy performance while sharing dated samples of a child's literacy activities and a record of the child's literacy performance on assessments over time. Keeping a record of a child's performance on specific literacy-related tasks can help a parent, teacher, and/or the child select the most beneficial activities for continually improving literacy skills.

When there are concerns about a child's performance on specific literacy tasks, parents are encouraged to talk with the teacher about specialists available at your child's school or someone who collaborates with the school who may provide more in-depth assessment information. A literacy assessment specialist should communicate with the family and teachers to identify alternative strategies that can be introduced to collaboratively support your child's literacy development.

A child who is struggling needs a team of parents and educators who communicate regularly to build on the child's strengths while nurturing the child's literacy needs.

Ask Questions about Tests
Parents and teachers are encouraged to discuss the following questions about formal, standardized tests. These questions help clarify, support, and verify how a child's daily performance may be linked to performance on a more formal test.

- *What is the full title and purpose of the test?* Most standardized tests provide an overview of class or school performance, but few offer specific diagnostic information. Individually-administered diagnostic tests given by trained teachers or specialists have more potential for identifying a child's specific literacy strengths and needs.

- *What skills are tested?* Reading vocabulary, comprehension, and spelling are examples of literacy skills often assessed on group-administered, formal standardized tests. Tests that assess subject-related knowledge in math, science, social studies, and other subjects will also require literacy skills. For example, word problems in math require a child to think and read. When reviewing a child's performance on a test, parents and teachers need to consider, "What literacy skills do children need to perform well on this test?"

- *How are literacy skills tested?* Vocabulary, comprehension, and word recognition may be tested in different ways, depending upon test authors and publishers. For example, comprehension sections on some tests require a child to read brief passages and answer questions. Other tests assess vocabulary and comprehension by having a child fill in the blanks in sentences. When reviewing a child's test scores, parents and teachers should consider how the skills were assessed and should ask, "What can we do at home and in school to help the child build on the literacy strengths while guiding them to improve literacy needs?"

- *How are the scores determined, interpreted, and used?* Norm-referenced and standards-based (criterion-referenced) tests are two types of assessments. Norm-referenced test scores reflect performance in comparison to a "norm group"—a group of students similar in age and/or grade.

  A child's norm-referenced score may be reported as a percentile. Many parents think that percentiles represent the percentage of correct answers. A percentile score actually represents how a child ranks compared to other children in the "norm group" who took the same test. For example, a fourth-grade student scoring in the 60th percentile on a nationally-normed test ranked better than 60% of the fourth-grade students participating in the national norm group.

A standardized test is any form of test that (1) requires all test takers to answer the same questions, or a selection of questions from common bank of questions, in the same way, and that (2) is scored in a "standard" or consistent manner, which makes it possible to compare the relative performance of individual students or groups of students.
Glossary of Educational Reform
(edglossary.org/standardized-test/)

There are two main types of assessment: summative and formative. Summative assessment occurs after instruction in the form of a multiple choice test or final exam that indicates the level of knowledge that the student has attained (Woolfolk, 2013). Formative assessment, on the other hand, occurs both before and during instruction. The purpose is to guide the teacher in planning and preparing the lesson and improving student learning.
Coen (2014) https://epdf.pub/
approaching-difficulties-in-literacy-
development-assessment-pedagogy-
and-program.html

Grade-equivalency or grade-level scores are often identified in norm-referenced test results. Parents need to beware of misinterpreting grade-level scores, because they are estimated comparisons to the norm group and do not specify a grade and month of a child's actual performance.

Standards-based (criterion-referenced) test scores reflect how a child meets the objectives or standards related to specific skills such as those identified in the Common Core State Standards. (http://www.corestandards.org)

Laura Slover and Lesley Muldoon highlight some of the key changes since the implementation of Common Core testing in 2010 in their 2018 article "How the Common Core Changed Standardized Testing." https://www.educationnext.org/common-core-changed-standardized-testing/: *One of the most important features of state tests today is their focus on college and career readiness. Unlike in the past, tests now measure a broad range of knowledge and skills that are essential to readiness and report students' progress toward that goal. Tests of old, like the standards undergirding them, often fell short of measuring the most important knowledge and skills that are critical for being prepared for college and for work.*

Explore Different Approaches

Ability to function and be productive in the real world is the ultimate test. Some children are better test-takers than others. Some are less nervous, others more challenged, and still others see tests as games, especially with the implementation of technology-based assessments.

Parents and teachers are encouraged to observe and keep dated notes, videos, writing samples and other examples of a child's performance on daily literacy activities related to the skills and standards addressed on tests. Part 3 of this book introduces over 100 activities linked to K-5 Common Core State Standards and preschool measures developed in California and now used in other states.

PARENTS!

My primary reason for writing the first edition of *Family Time Reading Fun* over 20 years ago was because after many years as an educator, I saw first-hand how important it is to engage families in their child's learning experiences beyond regular parent-teacher conferences. A growing number of research studies explore the importance of the parent in a child's literacy development.

One memorable take-home project that motivated my 4th

To assess young children's strengths, progress, and needs, use assessment methods that are developmentally appropriate, culturally and linguistically responsive, tied to children's daily activities, supported by professional development, inclusive of families, and connected to specific beneficial purposes ...
NAEYC (2003) pp. 2–3 and Tabors (2008) p. 145

Another important finding in the literature is that literacy skills begin to develop before a child is even able to read. Often, language is the first building block to literacy. Parents have a significant role in the development of language skills as they are predominantly responsible for the language with which children enter formal schooling.
Connor, C. (2016) p. 130

graders when I taught for the Department of Defense School in Babenhausen, Germany was having children write stories on a specific theme related to what we were reading in class. I would type their stories to create a booklet for each student in my class to take home to share with their family. "Our World of Imagination" was one of the booklets. Parents said their children were excited and very motivated to read and write, so they could see their stories in a "book."

When I became a parent, my commitment to communicating with families about how important they are in supporting their child's learning was reinforced by many first-hand experiences with our children.

My personal experiences with our three children reinforced my goal to write the 1st edition of *Family Time Reading Fun* in 1998 as a follow-up to my first book, *The Reading Triangle: Parent, Teacher, Child.*

Our sons were in high school and our daughter was in college, but the most memorable stories came from their elementary school experiences.

Encourage children to share positive and negative experiences … with our promise to help and not judge them. This was reinforced when we moved to California from Michigan in the spring of 1988 where John would leave his Dearborn, Michigan, office to work with the Ford Motor Company Western Office. I was teaching part-time for the University of Michigan School of Education at the time of our move, and was grateful to be invited to teach at the University of California, Irvine soon after our move. Anne was in fourth grade. Our boys were finishing preschool. Anne was proud to wear her University of Michigan jacket, and the boys loved wearing their U of M shirts after we moved.

When we took Anne to register for school in Irvine, I was surprised to hear her say, "Mom, please don't put me in a GATE class again." I was shocked to hear her reason when I asked, "Why?"

She said, "I didn't want to tell you what my teacher said when I took the last spelling test before we moved. I was afraid you would be mad at me."

I asked her to please tell us and not worry that we would be upset with her, as long as she remembered what we had told her in the past: "Always tell the truth. If it is bad news, we'll work it out together, because we're a team."

Anne then asked me, "Mom, do you think I'm a stupid idiot?" I was shocked to hear her question. I responded "Absolutely not ... where did you hear those words?" She said that before she took the last spelling test before we moved, her Michigan teacher told the class, "Any stupid idiot can get 100 on this test." Anne said she was very sad, because she missed one word and was afraid to tell us that she was a "stupid idiot."

This experience reinforced my goals to share with parents, teachers, and others that we need to be aware that what we say and how we speak can have a strong impact on children, and we need to encourage children to tell us things that might embarrass them with the goal of helping and supporting them, knowing that we are one team!

Parents and teachers are important partners as they communicate to better understand children's strengths and needs. Trevor was in first grade when we received a call from his teacher to request a special conference. When we met the next morning, we were surprised to hear her suggest that we may be letting him drink too much before school. We asked why she thought he was drinking too much in the morning. She said, "When I ask children to copy the 'morning message' from the front board, Trevor always asks to go to the bathroom. He usually stays there so long that when he gets back, he doesn't have time to copy the message."

We told her we would ask Trevor. That afternoon, when he came home, I told him what the teacher had told us, and he said, "I'm so sorry, Mommy. I really don't have to go to the bathroom. My desk is in the back row, and I can't see the message to copy it." We shared this with the teacher and told her we would have his eyes checked.

After the teacher moved Trevor's desk to the front row and he was prescribed glasses by our optometrist, he copied the morning messages, and never asked to go to the bathroom. Trevor showed us that he had definite strengths as a problem-solver. He asked to go to the bathroom rather than struggle with his need to see the board and write the morning message!

Research shows parents are important in supporting literacy. Chritina Clark provides a research summary of "Why it is important to involve parents in their children's literacy development" in her January 2007 online article for the National Literacy Trust.

> **Note:** Because literacy is influenced by so many factors, it helps to always remember that parents, teachers, and children are a team. Parents are a great influence on children's learning and are encouraged to continually explore fun, everyday learning experiences that support a child's learning. The following section *Literacy Strategies: Activities with a Purpose* provides many fun literacy activities that are easy to prepare and support literacy at home, school, and in the real world.

The evidence about the benefits of parents being involved in their children's education in general, and their children's literacy activities in particular, is overwhelming. Research shows that parental involvement in their children's learning positively affects the child's performance at school (Fan & Chen, 2001) in both primary and secondary schools (Feinstein & Symons, 1999) . . . https://files.eric.ed.gov/fulltext/ED496346.pdf Clark, C.-National Literacy Trust (2007)

Literacy Strategies: Activities with a Purpose

Activities involve actions. Strategies are actions with a purpose. Over 100 *Family Time Reading Fun* strategies are aligned, as applicable, to kindergarten through 5th grade Common Core State Standards for English Language Arts & Literacy in History/Social Studies, Science, and Technical Subjects (http://www.corestandards.org/ELA-Literacy/).

Family Time Reading Fun strategies are introduced in five literacy categories similar to those found in the K-5 Common Core State Standards.

1. Reading: Foundational Skills

2. Speaking and Listening

3. Language

4. Reading: Literature and Informational Text

5. Writing

Parents, teachers, tutors, after-school providers, and others who support literacy learning should consider the following guidelines to assist in selecting the most appropriate strategies for children.

- Have fun! Choose activities children will enjoy while they are learning. Learning while playing is supported by those who developed the Common Core State Standards.

- Support communication and collaboration between parents and educators to identify learning goals and the most appropriate strategies for a child based upon literacy-related daily observations and age-appropriate assessments.

- Use evidence from daily observations and assessments to choose strategies in Part 3 that will build on a child's strengths and improve literacy needs.

- Respond to questions posed at the beginning of each of the five categories in Part 3 to choose strategies for a child.

The Standards define what all students are expected to know and be able to do, not how teachers should teach. For instance, the use of play with young children is not specified by the Standards, but it is welcome as a valuable activity in its own right and as a way to help students meet the expectations in this document. National Governors Association Center for Best Practices, Council of Chief State School Officers (2010) Common Core State Standards for English Language Arts & Literacy in History/Social Studies, Science, and Technical Subjects (2010) p. 6

Grade levels indicated for each strategy in Part 3 can be used to select strategies designed to support a child in addressing grade-appropriate *Common Core State Standards* identified in Appendix D.

Choose strategies that will "stress a strength and nurture a need" and will provide opportunities for each child to continually grow as a learner.

Reading: Foundational Skills

Reading Foundational Skills support a wide range of literacy skills for children from Kindergarten through 5th grade. Foundational Skills for Kindergarten and Grade 1 focus primarily on hearing and saying sounds in words and sentences (phonological awareness), learning the alphabet, and other concepts about print. Phonics, word recognition, and fluency are foundational skills that can support those in Kindergarten through Grade 5.

Consider the following questions to determine which of the *Reading: Foundational Skills* strategies can build on a child's literacy strengths and which strategies can support areas of greatest need. The questions below are adapted from the K-5 *Common Core State Standards for English Language Arts Reading Foundational Skills* (2010).

Print Concepts

Does the child...

✓ Demonstrate understanding of the organization and basic features of print? (Grades K-1) See *Alpha*, page 33.

✓ Follow words from left to right, top to bottom, and page by page? (Grade K) See *Green Means Go*, page 41.

✓ Recognize that spoken words are represented in written language by specific sequence of letters? (Grade K) See *Seeing and Saying Key Words*, page 54

✓ Understand that words are separated by spaces in print? (Grade K) See *Finger Walk*, page 39

✓ Recognize and name all upper- and lowercase letters of the alphabet? (Grade K) See *Make a Match*, page 50

✓ Recognize the distinguishing features of a sentence, such as first word, capitalization, ending punctuation? (Grade 1) See *Seeing Words and Sentences*, page 54.

A focus on results rather than means
By emphasizing required achievements, the Standards leave room for teachers curriculum developers, and states to determine how those goals should be reached and what additional topics should be addressed ... Teachers are thus free to provide students with whatever tools and knowledge their professional judgment and experience identify as most helpful for meeting the goals set out in the Standards.
National Governors Association Center for Best Practices, Council of Chief State School Officers Common Core State Standards for English Language Arts & Literacy in History/Social Studies, Science, and Technical Subjects (2010) p. 4

Children develop concepts about print through seeing print in the environment and observing people using print for various purposes. ... "Phonological awareness" is generally defined as an individual's sensitivity to the sound (or phonological) structure of spoken language. It is an oral language skill that does not involve print.
California Preschool Learning Foundations, Volume 1 (2008) pgs. 51 & 52

Phonological Awareness

Does the child...

✓ Demonstrate understanding of spoken words, syllables, and sounds (phonemes)? (Grades K–1) See *Silly Sounds*, page 60.

✓ Recognize and produce rhyming words? (Grade K) See *Drivn' to the Beat*, page 38.

✓ Count, pronounce, and segment syllables in spoken words? (Grade K) See *Clapping Machines*, page 36.

✓ Blend and segment or separate onsets and rimes of single-syllable spoken words? "Onset" is the initial letter-sound in the single-syllable word such as "c" in "cat." "Rime" refers to the letters usually starting with a vowel that follow the first letter-sound such as the "-at" in "cat." (Grade K) See *Breaking Up Is Hard To Do*, page 35.

✓ Add or substitute individual sounds (phonemes) in simple, one-syllable words to make new words? (Grade K) See *Silly Sounds*, page 60.

✓ Distinguish long from short vowel sounds in spoken single-syllable words? (Grade 1) See *Seeing and Saying Key Words*, page 54.

✓ Orally produce single-syllable words by blending sounds (phonemes) in spoken single-syllable words? (Grade 1) See *Silly Sounds*, page 60.

Phonics and Word Recognition

Does the child...

✓ Know and apply grade-level phonics and word analysis skills in decoding words? (Grades K–5) See *Mystery Word*, page 52.

✓ Demonstrate basic knowledge of one-to-one letter-sound correspondences by producing the primary sound for each consonant? (Grade K) See *In the Bag*, page 42

✓ Associate long and short vowel sounds with common spellings for the five major vowels? (Grade K) See *Seeing and Saying Key Words*, page 54

✓ Read common high-frequency words by sight such as *the, of, to, you* ... (Grade K) Recognize and read grade-appropriate irregularly spelled words? (Grades 1–3) See *Word Speed-Up*, page 65

✓ Decode words with more than one syllable? (Grades 1–3) See *Mystery Word*, page 52

✓ Use combined knowledge of letter-sounds, syllabic patters, and more to read accurately unfamiliar multisyllable words in context and out of context? (Grades 4–5) See *Shopping for Words*, page 58

Fluency

Does the child...

✓ Read emergent-readers with purpose and understanding? (Grade K) See *Do You Hear an Echo?* page 37

✓ Read grade level text with purpose and understanding? (Grades 1–5) See *Record It,* page 53

✓ Read with sufficient accuracy and fluency to support comprehension? (Grades 1–5) See *More Fun than One*, page 51

✓ Use context to confirm or self-correct word recognition and understanding, rereading as necessary? (Grades 1–5) See *Joking Around*, page 44

If you answered "yes" to questions that apply to a child at the grade level(s) identified, this may be an area of strength for the child. If you answered "no," it may be an area that needs support.

Use the grade levels indicated for each strategy to assist in selecting strategies designed to support the children in achieving Kindergarten through Grade 5 expectations identified in Appendix D.

These standards are directed toward fostering students' understanding and working knowledge of concepts of print, the alphabetic principle, and other basic conventions of the English writing system. These foundational skills are not an end in and of themselves; rather, they are necessary and important components of an effective, comprehensive reading program designed to develop proficient readers with the capacity to comprehend texts across a range of types and disciplines.
National Governors Association Center for Best Practices, Council of Chief State School Officers Common Core State Standards for English Language Arts & Literacy in History/Social Studies, Science, and Technical Subjects (2010) p. 15

ABC Book

Recognizing Letter Names and Letter Sounds

Materials

- stapler or tape
- blank paper stapled together or in a bound note pad or spiral pad
- letter cards(pages 31-32)
- crayons, markers, magazine or catalog pictures, scissors, glue

Grade Levels

- Kindergarten
- Grades 1–2

This fun activity can be completed in short ten- to fifteen-minute sessions over several weeks.

- Staple sheets of paper together to form a 26-page booklet or use a note pad or spiral pad with at least 26 pages.

- Help your child place the letter cards in alphabetical order, grouping upper- and lowercase cards together to form pairs.

- Guide your child in copying or pasting copies of each pair of letters near the top of each page.

- Ask your child's teacher the order in which letters and letter sounds are introduced in your child's class. Introduce letters in the alphabet book at approximately the same time they are being introduced in school to preview or review learning.

- Invite your child to cut out two or three magazine or catalog pictures that will represent the consonant and vowel sounds being introduced in class. For example, your child might cut out a "flower" and a "flag" for the consonant sound /f/ or the consonant blend /fl/. You might choose an "apple" or "cat" for /a/.*

- Invite your child to glue the pictures on the book page, write the word, and underline the key letter-sound.

  - Write the words below each picture, so the child sees the letter sounds in print.

  Invite your child to review letter sounds by "reading" images and words with you, other family members, and the teacher.

  *The "slashes" around letters prompt us to say the sound represented by the letter(s) and not the name of the letters.

The Lowercase Alphabet

Cut out and use these cards (or other flash cards) for alphabet activities.

a	b	c
d	e	f
g	h	i
j	k	l
m	n	o
p	q	r
s	t	u
v	w	x
y	z	

The Uppercase Alphabet

Cut out and use these cards (or other flash cards) for alphabet activities.

A	B	C
D	E	F
G	H	I
J	K	L
M	N	O
P	Q	R
S	T	U
V	W	X
Y	Z	

Alpha

Recognizing Letter Names

It's Bingo with a twist!

30 minutes

GET READY TO PLAY

- Invite your child to make two or more Alpha cards (one for each person playing the game).

- Lay out samples of uppercase and lowercase letters from pages 31–32.

- Ask your child to write a different letter in each square of each Alpha card. (Letters should be in different spaces on each card.)

- Cut out letters from pages 31–32 or print letters on small cards.

- Turn the uppercase and lowercase letters face-down in a pile.

PLAY ALPHA

- Turn over the top letter and ask your child to call out the name of the letter.

- Each player must use a place-marker over letters that are called.

- Play the game until a player covers five letters across, vertically, or diagonally.

- The first person who covers five letters shouts Alpha and wins the game!

Materials
- Alpha card (page 34)
- samples of uppercase and lowercase letters (pages 31 and 32)
- place-markers (pebbles, pennies, paper squares)
- colored marker
- pen or pencil

Grade Levels
- Kindergarten
- Grade 1

Alpha Card

A	L	P	H	A
		Alpha Free Space		

Breaking Up Is Hard to Do

Blending Onsets and Rimes* to Form Words

Choose single-syllable words related to areas of interest to your child, such as baseball (*bat, ball, champ* ...), gardening (*rake, rose, leaf* ...), or animals (*dog, cat, cow* ...).

Play *Breaking Up Is Hard to Do*.

- Ask your child to choose a category or area of interest from the lists you created.

- **Do not show the word lists to your child.**

- Say each word by pronouncing the "onset" (part of the word before the vowel) and then the "rime" (part of the word starting with the vowel and any consonants that come after.) Example: /b/.../at/, /r/.../ake/, /d/.../og/

- Ask your child to say the whole word you are "breaking up."

- Play the game with each word on the list.

When your child wants to play again, ask your child to think of words and try to break up words into "onsets" and "rimes" for you to put together.

*The "slashes" around letters prompt us to say the sounds represented by the letter(s) and not the name of the letters.

Materials
- word list with single-syllable, high-interest words
- sample lists of "onsets" and "rimes"

Grade Levels
- Kindergarten
- Grade 1

SAMPLE: BREAKING UP IS HARD TO DO: Onsets & Rimes

Theme: soccer		Theme: baseball	
1. b-all	6. n-et	1. p-itch	6. b-at
2. k-ick	7. l-eague	2. thr-ow	7. b-unt
3. g-oal	8. t-eam	3. r-un	8. c-atch
4. p-unt	9. b-ounce	4. b-ase	9. f-oul
5. sc-ore	10. w-in	5. h-it	10. g-ame

Theme: food and drinks		Theme: animals	
1. h-am	6. m-eat	1. d-og	6. fr-og
2. ch-eese	7. m-ilk	2. c-at	7. b-ird
3. j-uice	8. br-ead	3. f-ish	8. t-oad
4. ch-ips	9. fr-uit	4. sn-ake	9. d-uck
5. n-uts	10. t-ea	5. b-ear	10. b-ull

Clapping Machines

Hearing and Responding to Words and Syllables in Songs and Poems

Materials
• children's songs, poems

Grade Levels
• Kindergarten
• Grade 1

Favorite children's programs and videos often have songs your child likes to sing. Invite your child to choose songs and poems from audio and video resources you choose.

- Listen to the songs and poems with your child.

- Clap to each syllable in the words. (Mar-y had a lit-tle lamb. Lit-tle lamb. Lit-tle lamb …)

Have a good time. You can even get up and dance while you clap! After becoming "clapping machines," talk about the importance of listening for the beat and trying to clap with each syllable.

Do You Hear an Echo?

Reading and Speaking with Expression

Bring out the actor (and fluent reader) in your child.

- Choose a poem, limerick, joke, or tongue-twister to read aloud with your child.

    (Ask friends and teachers for suggestions. *Beware! Do not allow children to search online alone* for children's jokes, poems, and limericks. There are many deceptive websites.)

- Here is an example of a tongue twister that is fun to try:

Materials
- poem, limerick, joke

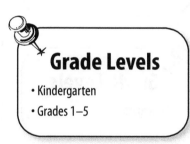

Grade Levels
- Kindergarten
- Grades 1–5

She sells seashells by the seashore

She sells seashells by the seashore;
　The shells that she sells are seashells I'm sure.

So if she sells seashells on the seashore,
　I'm sure that the shells are seashore shells.

- Read one line at a time with expression.

- Ask your child to repeat after you as your echo.

- Encourage your child to use the same kind of expression.

- Explore other tongue twisters or a joke or poem … as your child becomes your echo to build confidence and fluency!

Drivin' to the Beat

Hearing and Responding to Rhyming Sounds

Invite your child to choose favorite songs and poems with rhyming words.

Materials

- children's songs and poems with rhyming words

Grade Levels

- Kindergarten

- When you travel in the car, sing or recite songs or poems with your child.

- Make rhyming fun by leaving out a rhyming word as you sing.

- Invite your child to say the rhyming words you leave out at the end of a phrase or sentence.

Example:

I'm a little teapot
short and stout.
Here is my handle.
Here is my _____ (spout).

Parent leaves out "spout," so child can fill in.

Finger Walk

Spacing between Words in Sentences

10 minutes

Spacing between words and words in sentences is at your child's fingertips!

- Invite your child to begin writing the first word of a sentence on the top line at the left margin of a piece of paper.

- Show your child how to leave a space about the size of one or two fingers between each word.

- After writing a sentence, take a "finger walk" to check the spacing. Will one or two fingers fit between each word?

Encourage your child to space carefully, so others can enjoy reading what is written.

Materials
- writing paper
- pen or pencil

Grade Levels
- Kindergarten
- Grade 1

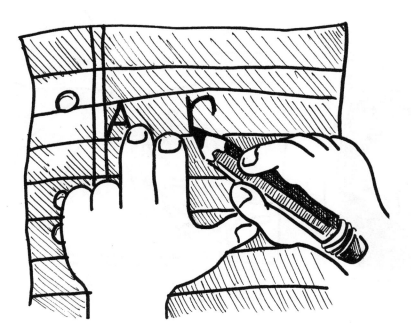

Fun on Board

Recognizing Letter Names

Turn riding in the car into quality alphabet time!

Grade Levels

- Kindergarten

- Invite your child to say the entire alphabet A–Z independently or with you.

- Ask your child to look for uppercase or lowercase letters from A-Z road signs, restaurants, license plates, billboards, or any word display.

- Invite your child to say "I see a(n) capital/uppercase- or lowercase __ on the (location)____"

- Continue the game through the entire alphabet, challenging all passengers to find all letters before reaching your destination.

Green Means Go
Writing from Left to Right

An important part of forming letters, words, and sentences is learning the direction in which to write. The "Green Means Go" activity is for beginning writers!

- Draw a green line along the left margin from the top to the bottom of the writing paper.

- Explain that the green line represents the word *go* or *start*.

- Show your child how to write from the green line (left margin) toward the right side of the paper.

- Continue by showing that you return to the left margin when you finish the first line of writing.

- Ask guiding questions as your child writes.

  - *Where are you going to start the first word?*

  - *In what direction will you go?*

  - *Where do you go when you finish writing on the first line?*

With a little practice, your child will go without the green.

Materials
- green marker
- writing paper
- pen or pencil

Grade Levels
- Kindergarten

In the Bag

Matching Beginning Letter Sounds to Objects

Materials

• consonant letter cards (pages 31–32)
• paper bag
• timer, tape

Grade Levels

• Kindergarten
• Grade 1–2

Try this lively alphabet game. The goal is to find in 10 minutes or less as many household objects as possible that contain a beginning consonant letter-sound.

● Place uppercase and lowercase letter cards in a paper bag. Your child's teacher can suggest appropriate letters to match letter-sounds currently being introduced at school.

● Set the timer for 10 minutes (or watch the clock).

● Shake the bag and invite your child to choose a letter without looking in the bag.

● Ask your child to name the letter and suggest words that begin with the sound represented by the letter. If your child has difficulty thinking of words, you may suggest a few words or your child can select another letter.

● Invite your child to search the house quickly to find an object that begins with the letter-sound represented by the letter. (For example, if your child chooses an "r," ask your child to name words that begin with the /r/ sound, such as "rabbit, run …" Then, invite your child to find something that begins with the /r/ sound, such as "refrigerator."

● Tape the letter to the object.

● Return to the bag to select another letter.

● When 10 minutes are up, count the number of objects correctly labeled with the consonants.

● Put all the letters back in the bag, and play again. Try to find more objects in 10 minutes with matching beginning letter-sounds.

Is It Too Hard?

Choosing Books that Support Fluency and Understanding

Do you ever find yourself asking, "Is that too hard for my child to read alone?" One or more of these strategies could help you gather evidence to discuss with your child and the teacher how to find reading material that will help your child develop fluency and understanding when reading.

PART 1: OBSERVE YOUR CHILD READING ALONE: WHAT PATTERNS OF BEHAVIOR DO YOU SEE?

- Does your child struggle frequently while reading words and sentences?

- Do you hear frequent excuses for avoiding the reading?

- Does your child hold the book in an awkward position—too close, too far, or at an unusual angle?

- Does your child wear prescribed glasses when reading?

- Does confidence change as the size of print or number of words on a page change?

Materials
- appropriate reading material for your child's reading level

Grade Levels
- Kindergarten
- Grades 1–5

PART 2: "FINGERS ON/FINGERS OFF TEST"

- Ask your child to read aloud approximately 50–75 words from a passage. (For example, the first paragraph on this page has approximately 50 words.)

- Ask your child to place a finger on the bottom of the page for each word that is challenging to read.

- If more than five fingers are "down" at the end of the passage, it may be too difficult for your child to read fluently and meaningfully.

- Don't abandon the challenging book! You and your child can enjoy it as you read it with your child.

Explore other "fluency" activities … and plan with your child's teacher which strategies are best when you and your child discover that something may be "too hard" to read.

Joking Around

Speaking and Reading with Expression

This activity will tickle your child's funny bone.

- Help your child choose several lively jokes from a joke book.

- Set up a puppet stage, such as covering a table with a blanket.

- Use markers or crayons to help your child make hand puppets from paper bags. (Use ready-made puppets, if possible.)

- Practice with your child taking turns reading and telling "Knock! Knock!" jokes or jokes from the joke book.

- Encourage your child to memorize the words and really "ham it up."

- Perform the jokes for family members and friends.

Materials

- joke book or children's "Knock, knock! Who's there?" jokes
- table
- table cover
- paper bags
- hand puppets made from paper bags, or ready-made puppets.
- markers/crayons

Grade Levels

- Kindergarten
- Grades 1–5

Land on It!

Recognizing Consonant Blends

Your child will "flip" for this fun game!

PART 1: GET READY TO PLAY

- Fill each space on the Consonant Blend Grid with a consonant blend* such as: bl, br, cl, cr, dr, fl, fr...

- Review the grid with your child (and other players who may join your child in playing) by saying a word which begins with each consonant blend.

- Ask your child to choose a timeline for playing "Land on It" and set a goal for how many words can be identified in a certain time limit (5, 10, or 15 minutes).

PART 2: PLAY "LAND ON IT!"

- You and your child take turns tossing a penny onto the grid.

- Each player names a word that begins with the consonant blend on the space where the penny lands.

- Write a word that your child suggests begins with the blend. If your child has difficulty thinking of a word, suggest two or three options and have your child select a word.

- Write the word that your child selects that begins with the consonant blend.

- Ask your child to read each word you wrote and underline the consonant blend.

- Continue playing until time is up. Count the number of words you and your child listed. Did your child reach the goal that was set for identifying a certain number of consonant blend words in the allotted time?

- Play again. Can you and your child think of more words in the same amount of time ... or should you suggest you change the timeline to name a different number of words in a longer or shorter amount of time?

* Consonant blends are two or three consonants in words that make distinct consonant sounds.

Materials
- Consonant Blend Grid, pg. 46
- penny
- pen or pencil
- writing paper
- timer

Grade Levels
- Grade 1

Consonant Blend Grid

Leave It Out

Predicting

Choose a picture book, article, poem, or nursery rhyme in which words and ideas are easy to fill in when you "leave it out."

- Read a passage to your child.
- Leave out a word that is important to the meaning of the passage.
- Invite your child to suggest a word that fits the meaning.
- Keep going when words are suggested that make sense.
- Stop briefly when the word does not fit the meaning.
- Suggest picture clues or the meanings and sounds of other words as clues to identify a meaningful answer.

Play "Leave It Out" from time to time to help your child think about meaning while reading.

Materials

- funny stories, poems, jokes, articles
- picture book, article, poem, or nursery rhyme

Grade Levels

- Kindergarten
- Grades 1–5

Letter Art

Matching Letter Sounds to Objects

Bring out the artist and reader in your child with this easy activity.

Materials

- letter cards (pages 31–32)
- crayons or markers
- blank paper
- glue
- small disposable objects

Grade Levels

- Kindergarten

- Ask your child's teacher the order in which letters are introduced in school.

- Choose a letter that is currently being introduced.

- Write the uppercase and lowercase versions of the letters in large print on a sheet of paper.

- Help your child search the kitchen or other places in and around the house for small, disposable objects that begin with consonants and short vowels represented by the letters, such as *sand* for *Ss*, *eggshells* for *Ee*, *leaves* for *Ll*, *macaroni* for *Mm*.

- Ask your child to cover the large written letters with glue, and place the small objects over the letters.

- Invite your child to say the name of the letter and the beginning letter-sound the small objects represent.

- Display the artwork after adding your child's name and the date.

Make a Game of It

Thinking About Questions and Answers

Help your child prepare to answer questions about stories they hear or read.

- Invite your child to carefully read aloud or listen to you read a small portion of the materials the teacher assigned to read at home.

- Give an answer to one of the possible questions the teacher may ask from what was read. (For example, read the nursery rhyme "Jack and Jill ran up the hill." Say, "Up the hill.")

- Ask your child to think of a question to match the answer. (For example, your child might ask, "Where did Jack and Jill run?")

- Give three or four more answers.

- Ask your child to think of a question for each one.

- Encourage your child to refer to the reading material, as needed.

- Continue with answers and questions until all material is reviewed.

Materials

- reading material from class assignment

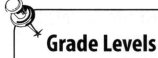

Grade Levels

- Kindergarten
- Grades 1-2

Make a Match

Matching Upper-and Lowercase Letter Pairs

Try a variation of "The Memory Game" to provide some alphabet practice.

Materials

• letter cards (pages 31–32)

Grade Levels

• Kindergarten
• Grade 1

PART 1: GET READY TO PLAY

- Pick out five or six upper- and lowercase letter card pairs. (Choose three or four letters your child knows well and two or three that are new or challenging.)
- Lay the cards face up in random order on the table.
- Invite your child to match the cards, offering help as needed.
- Turn the letter cards face-down in two columns, with the uppercase in one column and lowercase in the other.
- Mix up the letters within each column.

PART 2: PLAY MAKE A MATCH

- Ask your child to turn over one card from the left column and try to find the matching letter by turning a card over from the other column.
- If the upper- and lowercase letters that are turned over do not match, ask your child to turn both cards facedown again.
- If the cards match, your child keeps the cards.
- Play until your child matches 5 or 6 pairs of uppercase and lowercase letters.

If you want to play a second game, challenge your child to make the matches more quickly or add more pairs to the columns.

More Fun Than One

Reading and Speaking Smoothly with Expression

This activity proves that two can be more fun than one! Some words, phrases, and sentences are meant to be read (or sung) by several people at once. "Choral reading" includes more than one person sounding like one voice.

- Invite your child to choose a choral reading selection such as a poem, lines from a play, a joke, or a song to read aloud and perform using appropriate visual props.

- Ask your child to practice reading with you and others until the group sounds like one voice and uses the props appropriately.

- Encourage the rest of your family to join your child after the performance to sound like one voice.

- Choose a special time and date to perform.

- Capture the memory on camera!

Materials

- choral reading materials such as music lyrics, poems, play dialogue.
- optional: camera

Grade Levels

- Grades 3–5

Mystery Word

Blending Letter Sounds

Take a few minutes for some word fun!

PART 1: GET READY TO PLAY

Materials

- word list from one subject or theme
- markers
- paper strips
- book

- Make a list of five to ten "decodable" words from one subject area, theme, or story. (Decodable words are those words which have letter sounds which can be blended to form a recognizable word.)

- Write each word on the front of a paper strip leaving a space between each letter, letter sound combination, or syllable such as "d o g," "c a t," "sh ee p," "ap ple."

- Hide the strips in a book.

Grade Levels

- Kindergarten
- Grades 1–5

PART 2: PLAY "MYSTERY WORD"

- Talk with your child about the "mystery word" subject or theme.

- Gradually pull out the strip, so your child sees the first letter, letter combination, or syllable.

- Invite your child to suggest a word related to the "mystery word" subject area or theme that begins with the letter sound(s) or syllable that is revealed.

  - Pull out the strip a little further, so the next letter, letter combination, or syllable shows.

  - Encourage your child to continue blending the sounds and syllables as they are revealed to suggest a word that has the letter-sounds or syllables that are shown and that fits into the "mystery word" theme.

  - When the whole word is revealed, read the word and discuss how the word remained the same or changed as each sound or syllable was revealed.

  Play with each word strip. Your child will get some wonderful sound-blending practice!

Record It

Reading Words in Sentences Smoothly with Expression Can Improve Understanding

An easy way to help your child hear how reading sentences smoothly with expression instead of word-by-word can improve understanding is to "Record It."

Materials
- reading passage
- voice recorder
- optional: audio book

- Record yourself reading aloud from a passage of interest to your child or choose a passage from an audio book your child will enjoy.

- Invite your child to listen to your recording or the audio book passage and follow along in the written passage.

- After listening, discuss how reading smoothly helped your child tie all the words together to understand the story.

- Invite your child to record the passage to show how reading smoothly instead of word-by-word can improve understanding.

Grade Levels
- Kindergarten
- Grades 1–5

Seeing and Saying Key Words

Linking Word Sounds to Letters

How can you help your child with phonics at home?

PART 1: MAKE KEYWORD CARDS

Materials

- index cards
- scissors
- magazine cutouts
- glue
- thin-tip markers
- mall box or envelope

Grade Levels

- Kindergarten
- Grades 1–5

- Select one or two letter-sound combinations for your child to practice reading or writing. (Ask your child's teacher if you need help choosing combinations.) Combinations could include single consonants (b, p, d, m, ...), consonant blends (st, gl, tr, fr ...), consonant digraphs (ch, sh, th, ph ...), long/short vowels (a, e, i, o, u), vowel combinations (ea, ai, ee, ie), or r-controlled vowels (ar, er, ir, ur, or ...).

- Invite your child to think of a word that describes a familiar, everyday object that uses the letter-sound combination. (Examples: _blanket, car, beat_ ...)

- Write the word at the bottom of an index card.

- Underline the chosen letter combination.

- Invite your child to draw an illustration or find a picture in a magazine, cut it out, and glue it above the word on the card.

PART 2: DISPLAY KEYWORD CARDS

- Display the card where your child can see it when reading or writing.

- Make another card as your child is introduced to different letter combinations at school.

- Point to the cards to help when reading and writing new words.

- When working with vowel combinations, use various spellings and illustrations on cards that are clustered together to represent a single vowel sound. For example, for the long _a_, your child might make cards for _tail, frame, sleigh,_ and _tray_.

● Remove the card from the display area when your child shows confidence in applying a letter-sound combination when reading and writing. Store it in a "reminder box" or envelope.

Your child will look forward to seeing the cards go up and come down!

Seeing How We Read and Write Sentences

Reading left-to-right and recognizing beginning capitals and ending punctuation

Materials

• everyday reading selection—menu, alphabet book, program from sporting or other event

Grade Levels

• Kindergarten
• Grade 1

This fun activity can take place anywhere!

● Ask your child to follow along as you read an everyday reading selection.

● Point to key words and sentences. As you do, allow your fingers to flow from left to right under the words in a sentence. For example, when reading a menu, point to and read aloud food items from the children's menu. When attending a sporting event or theater presentation, point out the players' or performers' names in the program … sliding your fingers from left to right.

● When reading complete sentences, point to the first letter in the sentence. Ask your child, "What is special about this beginning letter?" Point to the ending punctuation and ask, "What is this called? Why is it important?" Explain the capitalization and ending punctuation, as needed.

● Repeat this activity from time to time when you are reading an "everyday something" together. It will help your child see how letters and words flow from left to right as we read, and sentences have special features.

Shop 'Til You Drop

Relating New Words to Real-World Objects

Shop 'til you drop with this real-world activity in the grocery store! Here are two possibilities:

- Invite your child to read words on signs, advertisements, and labels. For example, if you are in the produce section, point out and read the signs, *Bananas—$.59 a pound* and *Garden-fresh Tomatoes.*

- Play a food guessing game by giving a clue such as, *I'm thinking of a fruit that starts with the /b/ sound.* Point to the words as you pass them in the store, and invite your child to read the word.

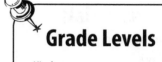

Grade Levels

- Kindergarten
- Grades 1–5

Shopping for Words

Identifying Words Using Real-World Clues

Materials
- writing paper
- pencil or pen

Grade Levels
- Kindergarten
- Grades 1–5

Need a good "reading" excuse to head for a shopping mall?

- Invite your child to help you make a list of five to ten words in various categories which could easily be seen while shopping. Words could include:

  DIRECTIONAL SIGNS = exit, pull, push, escalator, elevator, restrooms …

  CLOTHING STORE WORDS = sale, shirts, tops, dresses, skirts, pants …

- Invite your child to read the list out loud, or you may read it to your child before you enter the mall.

- Give the list to your child with a pen or pencil as you enter the store or mall.

- Challenge your child to find each word and check it each time it is found while you are shopping.

When you get home, talk about the various categories of words and where they were found. Congratulate your child for successfully shopping for words.

Shout It and Write It—I'm So Proud!

Hearing and Reading Positive Messages

Anytime

Help your child gain a positive attitude about learning by expressing your sincere pride in spoken and written words.

Materials
- schoolwork
- scrapbook

- Acknowledge your child's efforts and achievements by expressing your sincere pride in spoken and written words.

- Display work on a refrigerator, wall, or window with a special message from you attached. Ask your child to read what you wrote.

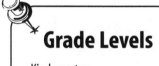

Grade Levels
- Kindergarten
- Grades 1–5

- Save your child's work and what you write to your child in an "I'm So Proud" binder. Date each piece of work. Invite your child to occasionally explore the "I'm So Proud" binder with you.

- These positive messages from you are rewards money cannot buy. Be sincere. Do not overdo praise or let it become an automatic reaction.

Show your child you are sincere when you say, "I'm so proud."

Silly Sounds

Substituting Sounds in Words

Silliness is the name of the game with this fun activity

Materials
• funny rhymes or poems

Grade Levels
• Kindergarten
• Grade 1

- Read to your child a variety of funny rhymes and poems with rhyming words such as those by Jack Prelutsky (*The New Kid on the Block*), Shel Silverstein (*Falling Up* and *Where the Sidewalk Ends*), and Hallie and Ruth Yopp.* Ask your child's teacher or search online for poetry and rhyme suggestions.

- After you read several poems aloud, choose words from the poems to "get silly with."

- Have your child get silly with the words by adding new beginning sounds (single phonemes or blends) to make real or nonsense words such as house, louse, pouse, shouse, fouse, and mouse.

- Invite your child to say as many new words as possible for each word you chose from the rhyme.

- To vary the game, play it on the road while driving and have your child make up new words from words that represent interesting things you see along the way.

By substituting phonemes (sounds in words), your child manipulates sounds, discovers new patterns in language, and enjoys a good laugh with you!

*Yopp, H. K., & Yopp, R. H. (2011). *Purposeful play for early childhood phonological awareness*. Huntington Beach, CA: Shell Education.

Tap Dancer

Hearing Words in Sentences

Read aloud to your child from some everyday reading material.

- As you read a sentence or phrase, ask your child to tap a foot as each word is read.

- Read the sentence or phrase a second time.

- Invite your child to tap again and count the number of words by counting aloud the taps. For example, if you read the phrase *And the cow jumped over the moon*, your child should tap seven times, one time as each word is read.

- When you read the phrase again, ask your child to say, *one, two, three, four, five, six, seven* as he or she taps.

Materials

- everyday reading materials (books, magazines, newspapers, nursery rhymes, poems)

Grade Levels

- Kindergarten

Trace-Over Art

Naming Letters in Words from Left to Right

Materials

- unlined paper
- glue
- colored ribbon or yarn
- scissors
- print or cursive alphabet
- pencil, pen, and/or markers

Grade Levels

- Kindergarten
- Grade 1

Use this "artsy" activity to increase your child's confidence in recognizing letters in familiar words, such as your child's name.

- Neatly print a familiar word such as your child's first name on a large piece of unlined paper.

- Ask your child to carefully say each letter from left to right and then slide a finger from left to right under the word to read the word.

- Ask your child to trace over each letter with glue, once again repeating the name of each letter.

- Invite your child to lay pieces of colored ribbon or yarn over the glue and repeat the letters and the word from left to right.

- Display the trace-over art for all to see.

Repeat the activity with other favorite words such as names of others in the family. Relatives love to receive "trace-over art" gifts on special occasions.

What a Character!

Reading Aloud with Expression

10 minutes

Invite your child to make a book come alive with this fun activity!

- Invite your child to help you select a familiar fairy tale, fable or story with various characters.

- Read the selection to your child.

- For each character, use a different voice and a great deal of expression.

- As you continue through the story, invite your child to choose a character to imitate.

- Ask your child to read what the character says, reading clearly and smoothly with expression.

- Change characters occasionally, so your child gets practice with other voices.

Use this activity from time to time when you and your child read a story with fun and interesting characters.

Materials

- familiar fairy tale, fable with dialogue such as Little Red Riding Hood, or a favorite story with various characters

Grade Levels

- Kindergarten
- Grades 1–5

Anytime

Wonderful Words

Telling the Truth in Love

Do you use "wonderful words" when discussing your child's schoolwork or any of your child's efforts?

Grade Levels

- Kindergarten
- Grade 1

- Speak honestly and respectfully; tell the "truth in love" by describing specific behaviors you noticed that demonstrated a strength and a need as your child completed a task. For example, your child took out the trash without being asked but forgot to close the gate to the yard, so the dog got out!

- Encourage your child to build on strengths (keep taking out the trash without being asked) and develop areas of need (remember to close the gate in the future).

- Invite your child to share with you what efforts and skills were needed to complete the task and what goals need to be set for the future.

Wonderful things can happen for your child when you know that your child is aware that you are using sincere "wonderful words" and setting future goals that stress a strength and nurture a need.

Word Speed-Up

Developing Memory and Word Recognition Skills

30 minutes

It's a race against the clock in this exciting word game.

PART 1: GET READY TO PLAY

- Help your child choose 12, 18, 24, or 36 words from a subject area, story, or everyday category (sports, popular music, food …).

- Write each word from the category on a small card.

- Place an even-numbered pile of cards face-down on each game board space.

- Set the timer for five or ten minutes.

PART 2: PLAY "WORD SPEED-UP"

- Toss a cube from a pair of dice or use a spinner with numbers from 1–6.

- Quickly pick up all the words on the space that matches the number on the cube.

- Invite your child to look carefully at the word, then read each word.

- Give the word to your child when it is read correctly.

- If your child has difficulty, read the word aloud, ask your child to look at the word again and repeat the word, then place the word face-down again on the numbered space.

- Ask your child to continue to toss the cube and read the words on the numbered spaces as they are revealed. If the space is empty because all words on a space were read correctly, read the words on the next space.

- Count the words read correctly when time is up.

- Review the words that were missed.

Materials

- list of words from textbooks, spelling lists, stories, or everyday topics
- small paper squares or cards
- game board (page 67)
- markers
- writing paper
- dice cube or spinner with numbers 1-6 on each side of the cube
- timer or clock with a second hand

Grade Levels

- Kindergarten
- Grades 1–5

PART 3: PLAY AGAIN

- If all the words were read correctly in five minutes, shorten the time to four minutes.

- If your child did not read some of the words, lengthen the time.

- Play the game until 18–30 words in the six piles have been read with confidence in 3–5 minutes.

Word Speed-Up Game Board

1	2
3	4
5	6

The Speaking and Listening Common Core State Standards require students to develop a range of useful oral communication and interpersonal skills. Students must learn to work together, express and listen carefully to ideas, integrate information from oral, visual, quantitative, and media sources, evaluate what they hear, use media and visual displays strategically to help achieve strategically to help achieve communicative purposes, and adapt speech to context and task.

Source: National Governors Association Center for Best Practices, Council of Chief State School Officers (2010) *Common Core State Standards for English Language Arts & Literacy in History/Social Studies, Science, and Technical Subjects* (2010) p. 8

Speaking and Listening

Consider the following questions as you observe children in K–Grade 5 to determine which of the following *Speaking and Listening* strategies can build on a child's literacy strengths and which strategies can support areas of greatest need.

The questions below were adapted from the K-5 *Common Core State Standards for English Language Arts & Literacy in History/Social Studies, Science, and Technical Subjects* (2010).

Speaking and Listening

Does the child . . .

✓ Engage in collaborative conversations? (Grades Kindergarten–5) See *Child Chat*, page 73

✓ Describe familiar people, places, things, and events and provide additional detail? (K–1) See *Play-by-Play*, page 84

✓ Add drawings or other visual displays to descriptions when appropriate to clarify ideas, thoughts, and feelings? (Grades K–1) See *Draw a Word*, page 74

✓ Include multimedia components (e.g., graphics, sound) and visual displays in presentations when appropriate to enhance the development of main ideas or themes? (Grades 2–5) See *Lights, Camera, Action!* page 80

✓ Ask and answer questions and make comments related to the topic of discussion? (Grades K–5) See *Career Field Trip*, page 71

✓ Express thoughts, feelings, and ideas clearly? (Grades K–5) See *Check Please!*, 72

✓ Differentiate between contexts that call for formal English (e.g., presenting ideas) and situations where informal discussions are appropriate? (Grades 4–5) See *News Reporter*, page 81

✓ Recount an experience with appropriate facts and details, speaking clearly? (Grades K–5) See *Going to the Doctor*, page 76

If you answered "yes" to questions that apply to a child at the grade level(s) identified, this may be an area of strength for the child. If you answered "no," it may be an area that needs support.

Use the grade levels indicated for each strategy to assist in selecting strategies designed to support the children in achieving Kindergarten through Grade 5 expectations identified in Appendix D.

Ask More and Tell Less

Taking Responsibility

Grade Levels
- Kindergarten
- Grades 1-3

When you ask more and tell less, you help your child get the job done and develop a sense of responsibility.

Ask

- What time are you supposed to meet the bus?

  Not... Remember to meet the bus at 8:00.

- What did I prepare for you to take to school today, so you won't be hungry in the afternoon?

  Not ... Remember to take your lunch and snack with you.

- What homework do you have today? How long do you think it will take?

- When will you clean your room today?

Confidence will grow at home and at school when your child starts putting into action the answers to your questions.

Career Field Trip

Explore Future Goals for Learning

Take a career field trip with your child, and it can help your child set learning goals now and in the future.

- Ask your child to name a career goal. Suggest possible choices by suggesting current careers of family members or close friends.

- Arrange visits to workplaces and personal meetings with family members, friends, or others in the profession(s) your child selects (e.g., teacher, firefighter, scientist, business person).

- Prepare your child by helping write a list of questions to ask.

- Encourage your child to read articles and other information about the profession before the visit.

- Encourage your child to ask the questions and listen carefully.

- If you cannot arrange a face-to-face visit, help your child write an email or letter to find out how people achieved their career goals.

- Encourage your child to ask what listening, speaking, reading, and writing skills are most important in preparing for their professions.

Materials

- writing paper
- pencil or pen

Grade Levels

- Kindergarten
- Grades 1–5

Check, Please!

Becoming a Confident Speaker

Grade Levels

• Kindergarten
• Grades 1–5

Try this fun activity to give your child practice in speaking fluently in public.

● Your child can be your voice as you run errands. Invite your child to:

• *Order food in a restaurant. When the family is ready to pay, encourage your child to politely ask the server, "May we have the check, please?"*

• *Ask where an item is located in a store and guide you to the location.*

• *Request directions when looking for something at the mall.*

● Congratulate your child on a job well-spoken!

Child Chat

Hearing, Understanding, and Using New Words

Grade Levels
- Kindergarten
- Grades 1–5

It's so easy!

Take 10-15 minutes or more at different times each day to talk with your child one-on-one … in the car, at the breakfast or dinner table … anywhere.

- Vary topics of discussion and introduce new words often as you speak. Topics could include sports, current events, travel plans, family news, hobbies, or family occupations.

- Ask questions that encourage your child to respond more in sentences … and less with "yes" and "no."

- Ask questions such as:

  - *What will you do if your friend cannot come to play with you today?*

  - *How do your friends celebrate during the holiday season in December and January?*

  - *What do you and your friends like to do to celebrate birthdays?*

  - *What would you do if you were asked to help a family who needs your help?*

  - *What do you do when you visit a family where they speak a language you do not understand?*

Listen carefully and make eye contact to show you are listening. Show you value your child's opinions and ideas.

A little chat will go a long way as your child begins to understand *and use* words when reading, writing, speaking … *and*, most important, you will learn more about your child's thoughts and feelings.

Draw a Word

Understanding School-Related Vocabulary

Materials

- lists of words that respond to questions you ask your child
- index cards
- timer or clock with a second hand
- drawing paper
- crayons
- markers

Grade Levels

- Kindergarten
- Grades 1–5

Turn a list of words about school into a "work of art" with this exciting game you can invite friends and family to play with you and your child.

PART 1: GET READY TO PLAY

- Choose 8–10 words your child can learn by answering two or three questions such as, "What did you learn at school today? What did you see at school? How do you feel?"

- Select words with one or more syllables ("mathematics," "reading," "thankful"), compound words ("football," "playground," "notebook"), words with prefixes ("unhappy"), and words with suffixes "cheerful."

- Choose words from different topics and different subject areas.

- Write the individual words on separate index cards.

- Invite your child to help you sort words into piles that answer each question you asked, such as, 1. "What did you learn in school today?" (mathematics, reading) 2. "What did you see at school?" (football, playground, notebook) 3. "How do you feel?" (sad, thankful, unhappy, cheerful))

- Place cards face down in a pile sorted by possible responses to the questions.

- Be certain you have enough drawing paper, so players can take turns drawing pictures on separate sheets of paper during the game.

PART 2: PLAY "DRAW A WORD"

- Gather a few friends or family members to form two teams to play "Draw a Word."

- Ask someone to be the timekeeper.

- The first player from one team chooses a word and reads the word silently. Do not show the word to anyone. (The player may ask someone on the other team for help in reading the word, if help is needed.)

- Start the timer when the player says, "Go."

- The player draws pictures to illustrate the meaning of the word. For example, if the word is "ocean," the "artist" might draw waves.

- Members of the artist's team try to guess the word that would answer one of today's questions: 1. What did you learn in school today? 2. What did you see at school? 3. How do you feel?

- Record the time it takes to guess the word.

- Continue to play until all words are guessed.

Add each team's total time. The team that takes the least time (smallest number) wins.

Going to the Doctor

Speaking Confidently with Purpose

Grade Levels

• Kindergarten
• Grades 1–5

Prepare your child to do most of the talking before visiting the doctor or dentist.

- Ask your child questions that the doctor or dentist might ask:

  - *Where does it hurt? How did you hurt yourself?*

  - *How are you feeling today? How long have you been feeling this way?*

- Help your child think of descriptive, accurate responses.

- Tell the doctor or dentist that your child would like to do the talking today.

- Feel free to help if your child needs support when explaining something.

Your child will get fluency practice and learn to give meaningful, accurate answers.

Hear It First

Improving Reading Comprehension through Listening

Sometimes a little exposure to a story in advance is all it takes for your child to understand. Use "Hear It First" when your child is reading a passage with new and challenging words and ideas.

- Invite your child to select a passage (a chapter or a few pages) from a school text that contains words and sentences that your child considers difficult to read and understand.

- Invite your child to listen as you think out loud … before, during, and after you read.

BEFORE YOU READ …

- Predict the content with your child by reading the title and discussing illustrations, charts, or other graphics.

- Tell your child what you hope to learn as you read the passage.

- Ask your child to be prepared to ask you questions about the passage when you finish reading.

WHILE YOU READ …

- Read the passage aloud, pausing occasionally to "think out loud" about what you are reading. Example: Share words and sentences that match or do not match your predictions. Share what you read that helps you learn what you hoped to lear from the passage.

Materials
- textbook passage or story
- sticky notes
- highlighter

Grade Levels
- Kindergarten
- Grades 1–5

AFTER YOU READ . . .

- After reading ... summarize aloud what you learned and how it matched or did not match your predictions.

- Invite your child to ask you questions.

YOUR CHILD'S TURN . . .

- Invite your child to share one or two of the most important questions to answer about the passage. (Write the questions down, so you can remember them later.)

- Ask your child to read the passage silently or aloud and mark words and important sentences that will help answer the questions.

- Invite your child to paraphrase or briefly retell what was read.

- Ask your child the questions written before reading the passage ... and add "who, what, where, when, and how" questions, as they apply.

"Hearing It First" should help your child better understand difficult passages!

Hide and Guess

Using Descriptive Language

What's the opposite of "Show and Tell"? It's "Hide and Guess." This is a fun game that builds an understanding of new words.

- Hide a small object in a paper bag (toy car, computer game, favorite little book).

- Gather the family or your child's friends to play.

- Ask your child to give one clue at a time which describes the object and answers some of the following questions:

  - *What does it look like?*

  - *How big or small is it?*

  - *What color is it?*

  - *Where do you usually see it?*

  - *How is it used?*

- Invite those who have gathered to ask other questions your child will answer to help them guess the name of the object.

- Encourage your child to use more challenging words each time you play, so your child's vocabulary can grow.

- Give other family members and friends an opportunity to hide an object and describe it, so others can guess.

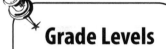

Materials

- paper bag
- small objects of interest

Grade Levels

- Kindergarten
- Grades 1-3

Lights, Camera, Action!

Responding to Words through Actions

Materials

- action songs, poems, nursery rhymes
- optional: camera or other recording device to capture the memory

Grade Levels

- Grades 2–5

Here's a simple 10-minute activity.

- Read aloud and act out the following action poem.
- Invite your child to watch the first time and then copy you as you read and act it out again.
- Practice the poem and other action poems until your child knows them from memory.

My Garden	Motions
This is my garden. I'll rake it with care.	*Extend one hand forward. Make a raking motion on palm with one hand.*
Here are the flower seeds I'll plant in there	*Make planting motions with thumb and index finger.*
The sun will shine and the rain will fall.	*Make a circle overhead with hands and then let fingers flutter down.*
And my garden will blossom and grow straight and tall.	*Cup hands together and extend slowly upward.*

Other action songs and poems can be easily located by searching online for "action songs and poems for children." Here is a sample:

All Kids

- http://www-personal.umich.edu/~pfa/dreamhouse/nursery/rhymes/

News Reporter

Writing, Reading, and Speaking Naturally

Family and school events are newsworthy. Invite your child to serve as a news reporter for a special event.

PREPARE THE NEWS ...

- Choose the event with your child.
- Invite your child to dictate or write a brief description of the event.
- Read the first draft of the report to your child.
- Rewrite the report together to make it sound like a news report.
- Help write the final version on poster board or paper. Use visuals or key words in large print as a "prompt" that can be seen and read from across the room.

DELIVER THE NEWS ...

- Invite your child to sit at the "news table" to read and/or recall from memory the news with a goal of sharing clearly and smoothly with expression, using appropriate props to support the news story (charts, weather maps ...).
- Gather the family for the "broadcast."
- Record the news report on a video recorder.

Just for fun, ask your child to make the report just before a family birthday or special holiday. Send the recording to relatives as a gift.

Materials

- first-draft writing paper
- writing paper or poster board that serve as "written prompts"
- tape to fasten writing prompts in front of News Reporter
- table
- video recorder

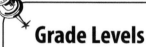

Grade Levels

- Kindergarten
- Grades 1–5

Last Saturday the Williams family attended their 15th annual family reunion.

Parent/Student/ Teacher Meeting

Setting Clear, Appropriate Expectations

Materials

- writing paper
- pencil or pen

Grade Levels

- Grades 1–5

When you or your child have questions about reading and writing and other school expectations, contact your child's teacher to request a parent/student/teacher meeting to discuss realistic goals.

PREPARE FOR THE MEETING . . .

- Ask your child to talk with you before the meeting to help make a list of questions to discuss with the teacher that focus on exploring school expectations.

- Bring the list of questions to share at the meeting.

DURING THE MEETING . . .

- Encourage your child to ask questions and enter into the discussion during the meeting.

- Look at work the teacher shares that your child completed independently at school. Also, look at some samples that needed support from the teacher.

- Share dated samples of reading and writing experiences your child completed independently from home, and share others you helped your child complete.

- Ask your child to join the conversation to discuss what learning is evident at home.

- Work together to create a list of strengths and areas that need to improve to meet expectations.

- Identify two or three goals that will build on your child's literacy strengths and support areas of greatest need.

- Ask the teacher to suggest ways you can help your child achieve the goals and grow as a confident and successful reader and writer.

AFTER THE MEETING . . .

- Write the goals you and your child identified at the meeting with the teacher.

- Post the goals that your child suggests. Give choices, if needed, such as on the refrigerator, in your child's bedroom ...

- Remember to always tell your child when you see her/him doing something to achieve the goals.

Play-by-Play

Learning and Using New Words in Context

Grade Levels

• Kindergarten
• Grades 1–5

It's so simple, yet so effective!

- Ask your child to give a play-by-play to tell what happened after watching a football or soccer game, a movie, or going to a party.

- Ask questions that guide your child to share the sequence of events. For example, if your child went to a birthday party, ask, "What happened when you arrived at the party? What did you do after that? When was the cake served?"

- Repeat in your own words or paraphrase what your child tells you to confirm that you heard and understood what was shared.

- Respond with sincere interest, using some new and different words with meanings that match what your child shared.

- Acknowledge your child when the new words are repeated and used during your child's discussions. For example, say, "Thank you for noticing that I used 'scampered' down the field instead of 'running'"

- Explain the meaning of new words as needed.

Occasionally, give your own play-by-play after sharing experiences with your child and have some fun pretending to speed up the commentary to act like real sportscasters.

Question and Answer Time

Improving Verbal Communication

Grade Levels
- Kindergarten
- Grades 1–3

How does your child respond when you ask, "How was your day?" or "What were some special things you did today?"

- Ask questions that encourage your child to think and use sentences with descriptive words.

  - *What did you do that made today so much fun?*

  - *What did you see in the movie that made it a comedy, a mystery, or an adventure?*

  - *What was something new you learned today?*

  - *What is so special about your best friend?*

  - *What would you like to do this weekend with the family?*

- Acknowledge and restate in complete sentences what your child says, so your child will know that you are listening and you understand.

- Encourage your child to ask you questions about your day.

- Respond in complete sentences with new words.

When you show interest by asking questions and answering your child's questions, you can help your child use new words and sentences in your future conversations!

Say It Like You Mean It

Practicing Voice Inflection

Material

• video or audio recorder

Grade Levels

• Kindergarten
• Grades 1–5

Have some fluency fun with phrases your child uses every day to describe likes and dislikes such as "This tastes good." "This is fun." "The movie was long." "May I have some more?" "May I be excused?"

● Ask your child to choose a phrase that will be part of a message to a friend, an oral presentation to give in class, a character in a book your child reads orally, or different characters in a play.

● Show your child how you would say a phrase three different ways. Then, ask your child to repeat the phrase in three different ways.

1. First, invite your child to say it like a question.

2. Second, ask your child to say it happily with a tone of excitement.

3. Third, ask your child to say it with a "sad" tone.

● Encourage your child to have fun saying other phrases and sentences in different ways, and record each effort.

● Discuss what you hear and possibly see in the recording.

● How does the same phrase change meaning as the tone changes?

Encourage your child to "Say It Like You Mean It," so anyone who is listening will understand the true meaning of the words.

Take Charge

Setting Goals

Encourage your child to Take Charge of learning and set goals when report card time rolls around, test results arrive in the mail, or an assignment was recently scored or graded by the teacher.

- Invite your child to meet with you at a special time to discuss test scores, grades on a report card, or a recent piece of schoolwork that was graded by the teacher.

- Look through your selection and make a list of "strengths" and "needs." The "strengths" are expectations that your child met, and the "needs" are areas that need to improve.

- Write one or two goals using the list of strengths and needs. The goal(s) should help your child build on strengths and improve areas that most need to grow.

- Write the goal on an activity planner such as the one on page 88.

- Encourage your child to choose activities that will help achieve the goal(s) and improve learning.

- Write the activities on the activity planner for your child, or ask your child to fill in the planner.

- Ask questions to explore progress in achieving the goal:

  - *What did you learn with that activity?*

  - *What evidence did you see that showed you were meeting your goal?*

  - *What would you do differently next time?*

  - *What would you do the same?*

- Store the activity planners in a file folder to show growth over time.

Materials
- activity planner (page 88)
- file folder
- test scores or report card, or a graded assignment

Grade Levels
- Kindergarten
- Grades 1–5

"Take Charge" Activity Planner

Name _____   Date _____

Goal: I will _____

What are three activities that will help me achieve my goals?

1. _____

   _____

2. _____

   _____

3. _____

   _____

	Date Begun	What I Did	Date Completed	Evidence That I Achieved My Goal
Activity One				
Activity Two				
Activity Three				

Tell Me More

Gaining a Sense of Accomplishment

Don't just tell your child that you like something; tell why!

- Sincerely acknowledge an accomplishment when your child completes a task.

- Avoid generalities such as "good job."

- Be specific.

  - *Thank you for taking the trash out without being reminded. How does it feel when I don't remind you?*

  - *I see that you looked at the clock and began doing your homework at 4:30. How does it feel to be finished before dinner?*

  - *Thank you for putting your toys away. How do you think what you did makes me feel? How does it make you feel?*

- Invite your child to paraphrase or repeat what you are acknowledging to confirm that the positive message was heard and understood.

- Occasionally, take a photo of an accomplishment to save the memory.

Feeling a sense of accomplishment can encourage your child to complete tasks at home and at school.

Materials

- camera

Grade Levels

- Kindergarten
- Grades 1–5

Language

Consider the following questions as you observe children in K-Grade 5 to determine which of the following *Language* strategies can build on a child's literacy strengths and which strategies can support areas of greatest need.

The questions below are adapted from the K-5 *Common Core State Standards for English Language Arts & Literacy in History/Social Studies, Science, and Technical Subjects* (2010).

Language

Does the child . . .

✓ Produce and expand complete sentences in everyday language activities? (Grades K–4) See *Sentence Scramble*, page 108

✓ Use knowledge of language and its conventions when writing, speaking, reading, or listening? (Grades 2–5) See *Story Words*, page 110

✓ Produce complete sentences appropriate to the task and situation? (Grades K–5) See *Taking Turns*, page 111

✓ Understand real-life connections between words and their use? (Grades K–3) See *Demonstration Station*, page 99

✓ Spell grade-appropriate words correctly? (Grades K–5) See *Shake It. Make It.,* page 109

✓ Identify real-life connections between words and their use? (Grades K-3) See *Wish Lists*, page 115

The Language standards include essential "rules" of standard written and spoken English, but they also approach language as a matter of craft and information choice among alternatives. The vocabulary standards focus on understanding words and phrases, their relationships, and their nuances and on acquiring new vocabulary, particularly general academic and domain-specific words and phrases.

Source: National Governors Association Center for Best Practices, Council of Chief State School Officers (2010) *Common Core State Standards for English Language Arts & Literacy in History/Social Studies, Science, and Technical Subjects* (2010) p. 8

(continued next page)

If you answered "yes" to questions that apply to a child at the grade level(s) identified, this may be an area of strength for the child. If you answered "no," it may be an area that needs support.

Use the grade levels indicated for each strategy to assist in selecting strategies designed to support children in achieving Kindergarten through Grade 5 expectations identified in Appendix D.

At Close Range

Forming Letters and Words

Build confidence forming letters and words by copying at close range:

- Invite your child to choose a list of words or brief sentences you will write on one piece of paper and invite your child to copy on another. Suggest words such as "to-do list," word list from school subject, "wish list," or a sentence expressing a special message. For example, "I love my dad."

- Write words or sentences as your child dictates using the form of letters your child uses in school. Write on every other line.

- Invite your child to copy each word and/or sentence on the same paper or different paper directly below the words or sentences you wrote. When copying on a different piece of paper, place the papers close together, so your child can clearly see the words to be copied.

- Encourage your child to form letters and words the way you wrote them using print used in school or on page 96.

- Write dates on each writing sample.

- Keep the writing samples in a folder, so you will see writing grow over time.

Materials

- writing samples
- lined paper similar to the paper used at school
- print or cursive alphabet (page 96)
- file folder
- pencil or pen

Grade Levels

- Kindergarten
- Grade 1

Call It as You See It

Describing Writing Strokes

Materials

- writing paper
- pencil or pen

Grade Levels

- Kindergarten
- Grade 1

Call it as you see it, so your child can listen and learn to write.

GET READY ...

- Choose letters your child is learning to write in school.
- Use the same type of writing paper as that used in school.

YOUR TURN ...

- Talk aloud as you write the letters. Talk about how you form the letters, and describe the strokes you make to form the letters. "Straight down ..." "Straight across ..." "Two humps ..." "Around ..." "Curve ..."
- Use terms that are familiar to you and your child. Ask your child and the teacher if there are terms that are used in school.

YOUR CHILD'S TURN ...

- As your child writes, encourage your child to describe the strokes needed to form the letters. Use the same terms you used.

Be consistent with using words your child will understand while growing as a writer.

Charted Letters

Forming Words and Letters Correctly

30 minutes

Chart letters, so your child can grow as a writer.

PREPARE CURSIVE OR PRINT CHARTS . . .

- Choose an alphabet that matches what your child is expected to write in school—print or cursive.

- Write uppercase and lowercase letter pairs in large print or cursive on 26 different pieces of paper.

USE THE LETTER CHARTS AS EXAMPLES . . .

- Invite your child to help you display the letter charts where your child can see them when writing.

- Write on the charts the correct form of words that your child needs for reminders (such as words with letters that are sometimes reversed, names of family members ...)

- Remind your child to use the charts as a model of how to form letters and words.

ADD WORDS AND REPLACE CHARTS...

- Add words to the charts from time to time.

- Replace the charts when your child learns to write the words without a need for the reminder.

Materials

- print or cursive alphabet (page 96)
- blank paper
- markers
- tape

Grade Levels

- Kindergarten
- Grade 1

The Alphabet in Print

Refer to this alphabet (or one provided by your child's teacher) for printing activities.

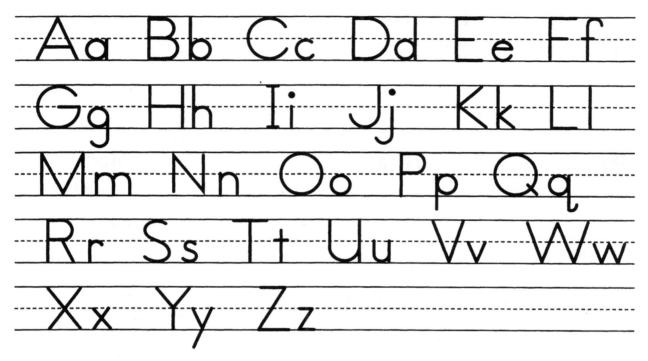

The Alphabet in Cursive

Ask the teacher when cursive is taught in your child's school. If your child is learning cursive, refer to this alphabet (or one provided by your child's teacher) for writing activities.

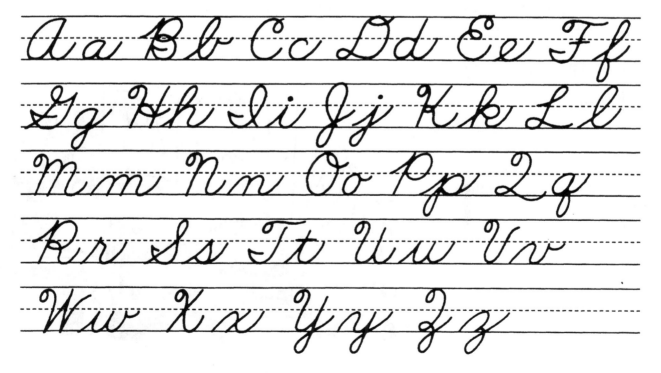

Cleaning Day Fun

Connecting Words and Their Meanings

Cleaning and learning can happen together with this fun, educational activity!

- Ask your child to help you gather a pile of clothing, toys, sports equipment, or art supplies.

- Invite your child to sort the items into "broad" categories first: clothes, toys, etc.

- Display a list of two or three categories.

- Ask your child to name each item in a specific category and choose a storage container or other area that will be large enough for items to be stored.

- Help your child write the name of each specific category on labels to identify where items will be stored (shelves, drawers, boxes, file folders).

- Place the labels on the storage areas or containers.

- Encourage your child to put things away using the labeled containers.

- Help your child go through the storage areas occasionally to see that the items are correctly placed. Are other storage containers needed?

- Add labels, as needed, on other storage areas.

Materials

- children's everyday items (clothing, toys, sports equipment, art supplies)
- storage units (dressers, shelves, milk crates, cardboard boxes)
- file folders
- labels
- washable markers

Grade Levels

- Kindergarten
- Grade 1

Computer Fun with New Words

Learning Word Meanings Using Computer Tools

Materials

- picture book or article
- writing paper
- computer
- word-processing software with a thesaurus and dictionary
- online dictionary and thesaurus

Grade Levels

- Kindergarten
- Grades 1–2

Hop on the information superhighway *with your child* to help your child speed into understanding and using new words. Parents need to *always* monitor their children closely when children are online

- Read aloud from a book or article with your child.

- Help your child choose four or five "new" words that are important to understanding and remembering the key information from the book or article.

- Invite your child to type the words and save them.

- Explore with your child an online dictionary or thesaurus to look up the meaning(s) and/or a synonym for each word. Helpful web sites are: www.m-w.com or www.wordcentral. com. (These web sites are maintained and supported by the Merriam-Webster Dictionary.) (See Appendix B for other online resources.)

- Read the definition or synonym from the online/computer dictionary or thesaurus. Copy and "paste" and/or type the definition/synonym next to the words typed earlier.

- Invite your child to create a picture dictionary using graphics from online resources or software as reminders of the definitions and synonyms that were recorded. Online graphics are available on the web by doing a search for "free vocabulary pictures," "free graphics," "free picture dictionary," and other similar key word searches.

- Print out and display the words, definitions, and graphics.

Choose other books and articles to keep having Computer Fun with New Words!

Demonstration Station

Completing Each Step of an Assignment

Help your child learn by seeing and doing things in the real world.

- Choose important everyday activities such as preparing a recipe, fixing a flat tire, or gardening.

- Invite your child to watch and help while you complete the activity.

- Describe what you want to accomplish and explain each step as you work.

- Review the steps after your demonstration.

- Ask your child to help you achieve your goal.

- Explain that an important part of organization for school is completing each step of an assignment, just as you did in the real-life demonstration.

- Invite your child to join you regularly in completing tasks that lead to achieving a real-world goal.

Book Cooks by Cheryl Apgar (Creative Teaching Press-2002) has easy-to-follow recipes linked to popular children's books. For example, "Butterfly Bites" is a favorite linked to *The Very Hungry Caterpillar*.

Materials

- items for completing a short real-world task such as preparing a recipe, fixing a flat tire, gardening
- writing paper
- pencil or pen

Grade Levels

- Kindergarten
- Grades 1–3

Down to a System

Getting Organized

Do you hear "Have you seen my homework?" Try this.

Materials

- small storage containers (cardboard or plastic)
- file folders
- notebooks with dividers
- labels
- backpack

Grade Levels

- Kindergarten
- Grades 1–3

- Set a time to meet and help your child organize a study area and backpack.

- Invite your child to gather and clearly label several small storage containers for the study area. Prepare labels for supplies such as crayons, pencils, papers, markers …

- Ask your child to select and label pockets and other storage areas in the school pack for lunch money, notes, homework … using appropriate sizes, shapes, and a logical pattern of how materials are organized.

- From time to time, help your child take inventory and put things back in order.

Your child will soon understand that a little time beforehand will save a lot of time later!

Far, Far Away

Copying Letters and Words from a Distance

Writing messages near and far can be helpful to those who send and those who receive.

- Write a grocery list, telephone message, or other information on a message board using print or cursive as used in your child's classroom.

- Place the message on the wall across from where your child sits to write.

- Ask your child to copy the grocery list or message onto paper.

- Encourage your child to form the letters and words correctly.

- Take the list to the store or give the message to the person for whom it is intended.

- Invite your child to practice copying from a distance in the same way copying from a distance is expected in the classroom.

Materials

- print or cursive alphabet (page 96)
- paper
- message board
- pen or pencil
- markers

Grade Levels

- Kindergarten
- Grade 1

Feeling Good!

Feeling How Letters, Numbers, and Words Are Formed

Materials

- sand, table salt, or shaving cream
- cake or pie pan
- index cards
- markers

Grade Levels

- Kindergarten
- Grade 1

Your child can feel good about writing with this activity.

- Cover the bottom of a cake or pie pan with sand, table salt, or shaving cream.
- Ask your child to choose letters, numbers, or words to practice writing.
- Write large letters or words on an index card.
- Invite your child to name each letter or read the words.
- Place a card next to the cake pan which is in front of your child.
- Ask your child to use a finger from his/her writing hand to copy the letter or word in the pan.
- Encourage your child to say the letters as they are formed.

Play whenever your child wants to "feel good" about writing letters and words.

Not-a-Bore Chore

Becoming Actively Involved in Learning

Household chores are excellent learning opportunities!

- Choose a chore new to your child, such as weeding the garden, emptying the trash, or sorting the mail for different members of the family.

- Demonstrate the chore as you share with your child how to do it. Use words and concepts to describe the chore.

- Invite your child to describe how to complete the chore and acknowledge your child when using key words related to the chore.

- Discuss why the chore is important to your family and why the sequence you demonstrated was beneficial.

- Your child will grow more positive and confident by making an important contribution to the family.

Materials

- childhood chore

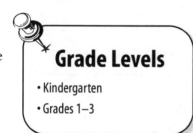

Grade Levels

- Kindergarten
- Grades 1–3

Personal Speller

Improving Spelling When Writing

A "personal speller" will help your child remember how to spell new words when writing.

Materials

- blank page and a stapler or a spiral notebook with at least 26 pages
- markers
- pencil or pen

Prepare the Speller...

- Staple 26 blank pieces of paper together or use a spiral notebook with at least 26 pages.

- Ask your child to write an uppercase and lowercase letter of the alphabet (Aa-Zz) at the top of each page.

Grade Levels

- Kindergarten
- Grades 1–5

Use the Personal Speller...

- Invite your child to ask for help spelling a few key words when writing a letter, a story, or a report.

- Ask your child to open the "personal speller" to the page with the first letter of the word to be spelled.

- Guide your child to the correct page if the letter-page selected by your child is incorrect.

- Write the word on the correct page.

  - Encourage your child to use the "personal speller" during each writing experience.

Picture What You Mean!

Matching Words to Picture Definitions

It's word meaning fun for everyone when you make and play "Picture What You Mean!" Invite your child to help you make "word cards" and matching "picture cards" from various topics to play this game.

PART 1: MAKE WORD CARDS AND PICTURE CARDS

- Choose five to six key words your child will need to answer questions you might ask about a story, a subject area, or an everyday area of interest.

- Choose some words with prefixes and suffixes that change the meaning of a word. Examples: happy, unhappy, happiest

- Write the selected words on each of the word cards.

- Invite your child to draw a picture or cut & paste pictures on picture cards to match each of the words.

30 minutes

15 minutes

Materials

- index cards
- markers
- optional: pictures from catalogs and magazines, scissors, and paste/glue

Grade Levels

- Kindergarten
- Grade 1

PART 2: MATCH PICTURES

- Place the cards face up.

- Invite your child to match the pairs of word cards and picture cards as quickly as possible.

PART 3: PLAY "PICTURE WHAT YOU MEAN!"

- Turn the picture cards face down. Mix up the order as you place them in a row.

- Turn the word cards face down. Mix up the order as you place them in a row next to the picture cards.

- Invite your child to turn over one card from the word row, and read the word.

- Ask your child to try to find the matching picture card from the picture row.

- If your child turns over a match, your child can keep the pair of cards and take another turn.

- If your child does not turn over a matching pair, turn the cards face down in the same place. Remind your child to remember where words and pictures cards are located.

- Take turns until all matches are made.

Rainbow Word Trace-Over

Exploring Letter Formation

Create a colorful writing experience.

- Invite your child to choose a few lines from a favorite poem or nursery rhyme or a sentence from a favorite story.

- Invite your child to watch as you write the selection on lined paper … similar to what your child uses at school.

- Write each word in a different color to show one word from another.

- Invite your child to trace over each word in another color to form a "rainbow word."

- Write the date on the writing sample.

Keep dated samples in a file folder to watch your child's writing grow.

Materials

- poem or nursery rhyme
- lined paper
- print or cursive alphabet (page 96)
- writing samples
- markers
- file folder

Grade Levels

- Kindergarten
- Grade 1

Sentence Scramble
Creating Meaning from Words

This game is easier than making scrambled eggs and is a great way to help your child become a strong reader.

Materials
- story or article of interest to your child
- index cards
- colored markers

Grade Levels
- Kindergarten
- Grades 1–5

PREPARE TO SCRAMBLE . . .

- Ask your child to help you choose two or three important sentences from a passage you read to your child or that your child read independently.
- Use a colored marker to write on index cards each word from the first sentence selected.
- Capitalize and use other correct punctuation when writing words from each sentence on the index cards.
- Use a different colored marker for words in each of the other sentences that are selected.
- Place words from each sentence in order on the table.
- Invite your child to read the sentences.

SCRAMBLE AND UNSCRAMBLE . . .

- Scramble the cards, so the words are out of order.
- Ask your child to unscramble the words to form a sentence from the reading passage.
- Repeat the activity with the other sentences.

A CHALLENGE . . .

- Make the activity more challenging when your child is ready.
- Ask your child to put the sentences in the order in which they were used in the story or article.

If your child enjoys a little competition, record the time it takes to unscramble a sentence. Challenge your child to unscramble the sentence again in less time.

Shake It. Make It.

Building New Words

Avoid hearing *I'm bored!* Play this fun make-a-word game.

- Write a lowercase letter of the alphabet on each side of nine wooden cubes (found in most craft stores).
- Write the alphabet twice. (Choose two letters to write three times.)
- Juggle the nine cubes in a can or similar container.
- Dump the cubes on the table.
- Use the letters that are face up to create as many words as possible.
- Write a list of words created by your child from the letters that were face-up.
- Play as many times as you like to try to create a longer list of words each time.
- Check grade-appropriate dictionaries, as needed, to confirm spelling. (See online dictionaries in Appendix B.)

Time will fly and your child will learn new words!

Materials

- nine wooden cubes
- thin-tip marker
- writing paper
- can or similar container to hold cubes

Grade Levels

- Kindergarten
- Grades 1–5

Story Words

Using Nouns to Create Stories

This game changes every time you play it!

Materials

- blank index cards or small picture cards with familiar objects
- markers
- paper bag
- timer/clock with a second hand
- audio/voice recorder

Grade Levels

- Kindergarten
- Grades 1–3

PREPARING THE STORY WORDS . . .

- Help your child think of several nouns (people, places, things) or choose picture cards with items of interest. The nouns can be real (such as "fish") or imaginary (such as "dragon").

- Write each word your child dictates on a blank card or invite your child to name pictures/illustrations on picture cards.

- Place the cards in a paper bag.

PREPARING TO TELL THE STORY . . .

- Invite your child to choose three word or picture cards from the paper bag.

- Invite your child to read the word cards or name the object on the picture cards. Help your child read the words, if needed.

- Explain that your child may have one or two minutes to think of a story that includes the three words.

- Challenge your child to think and not speak. "Practice the story in your mind."

- At the end of one minute, ask if your child would like one more minute to "practice."

TELLING THE STORY . . .

- At the end of the one or two minutes, ask your child to tell the story as you record it.

- Point to the words as you hear your child say them in the story.

- Write the story, so your child can read it now and in the future.

Encourage your child to take time to think about story words when planning to write a story in school.

Taking Turns

Speaking in Meaningful Sentences

It can be sentence fun in the car, sentence fun on a walk, sentence fun at the table. It's sentence fun anywhere!

- Start by saying the beginning of a sentence aloud. Examples:

  - *My favorite lunch is …*

    - *I love to go to …*

    - *My favorite memory with my family is …*

    - *I think the nicest thing to do for someone else is …*

- Invite your child to finish each sentence. For example: You might say, *My favorite memory with my family is …* Your child might say, *when we went camping at the state park.*

- Encourage your child to use words that make sense and form complete sentences.

- Guide your child to become more confident in forming complete sentences quickly and logically.

- Invite your child to suggest "sentence beginnings." Set an example by finishing these "sentence beginnings" with ideas and words that make sense.

The Right Fit

Finding the Right Writing Tools

Does your child have trouble forming letters and words? Sometimes the solution is as simple as changing writing tools!

Materials

- different-size pencils
- pencil grips
- markers
- unlined paper
- ruler

Grade Levels

- Kindergarten
- Grade 1

SELECT DIFFERENT SIZES ...

- Choose two or three different-size pencils, markers, and pens/pencils with plastic or rubber "grips" designed to help small fingers hold thin pencils/pens.

WRITE ...

- Invite your child to write his/her name two or three times using a different size marker, pencil, and/or pen each time.

OBSERVE ...

- How does your child's writing change? How comfortable is your child as a different marker, pencil, or pen is used?

CHANGE, AS NEEDED ...

- Use unlined paper with beginning writers who may be frustrated when trying to write on lines and between lines, regardless of the size of the writing tool.

- Suggest that your child change the size of the writing tool when it helps your child gain confidence and write legibly.

Encourage your child to find "The Right Fit!"

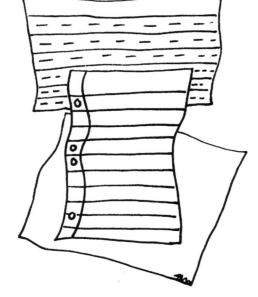

Thematic Picture Dictionary

Building Word Recognition and Understanding

This activity is just what your child needs to recognize and remember new words.

- Invite your child to choose a personal interest (such as sports, music, movies) or a subject area (science, math, social studies, art) or a special day (birthday, Valentine's Day, Thanksgiving).

- Use your child's choice as the theme for a personal dictionary.

- Staple blank sheets of paper together to form a 26-page booklet or use a notebook with 26 or more blank pages.

- Invite your child to write uppercase and lowercase letters in alphabetic order on each of the 26 pages of the booklet or notebook.

- Help your child begin by selecting approximately five important words that will help answer questions after reading and discussing a story, article, or other passage related to the theme that has been selected.

- Choose words your child wants to remember how to spell and understand when writing about what has been read.

- Ask your child to write each word on the page which represents the first letter of each of the words.

- Discuss what the word means in the story or article.

Materials

- stapler
- blank paper or notebook with paper
- books or magazine or news articles
- crayons
- markers
- scissors
- glue
- dictionary
- picture dictionary

Grade Levels

- Kindergarten
- Grades 1–3

● Guide your child to look up the meaning in a dictionary such as those available in the library, bookstores, and online:

Examples of dictionaries to support parents and children, including english learners (See Appendix B.):

- **Merriam-Webster Dictionary**
  http://www.m-w.com
  (Online dictionary and thesaurus for children and adults.)
  http://www.wordcentral.com
  (Online dictionary for children.)

● Guide your child to illustrate the meaning in some way. Draw a picture or cut and paste a picture from a magazine or newspaper advertisement that will remind your child of the definition.

● Keep working together on the theme until your child chooses another theme.

● Keep each Thematic Picture Dictionary in a special place where your child can get in the habit of using it when reading and writing.

Wish Lists

Relating New Words to Real-World Objects

What will keep your child happy and learning for hours just before a holiday or birthday?

- Invite your child to cut out pictures from catalogs or advertisements to form a "wish list"—a list of gifts your child would like to give to friends or relatives or wishes for your child's birthday gifts (that are within your budget).

- Ask your child to group related objects (toys, clothes, school supplies, music, computer software).

- Glue the pictures by category on different pieces of paper or one large piece of paper.

- Invite your child to describe each object by writing the name of the item and a short description next to each illustration.

- Discuss the wish lists with your child by asking …

  - How much do you think these cost?

  - Do these all fit in our budget?

  - Which ones will be the most important for your friends?

  - What will be important to remember when you give gifts to others in the future?

Your child can learn to read and write new words during this exciting time of the year by creating wish lists. Wish lists can also open the door for discussing how to remember other people during this exciting time … and throughout the year.

Materials

- catalogs
- newspaper
- magazine advertisements
- scissors
- glue
- blank paper

Grade Levels

- Kindergarten
- Grades 1–3

Through extensive reading of stories, dramas, poems, and myths from diverse cultures and different time periods, students gain literacy and cultural knowledge as well as familiarity with various structures and elements.

Reading Standards for Literature K-5 (RL) and Reading Standards for Informational Text K-5 (RI) offer a focus for instruction each year and help ensure that students gain adequate exposure to a range of texts and tasks. Rigor is also infused through the requirement that students read increasingly complex texts through the grades.

Source: National Governors Association Center for Best Practices, Council of Chief State School Officers (2010) *Common Core State Standards for English Language Arts & Literacy in History/Social Studies, Science, and Technical Subjects* (2010) pages 10-11

Reading: Literature and Informational Text

Consider the following questions as you observe children in K–Grade 5 to determine which of the following *Reading: Literature and Informational Text* strategies can build on a child's literacy strengths and which strategies can support areas of greatest need.

The questions below are adapted from the K–5 *Common Core State Standards for English Language Arts & Literacy in History/Social Studies, Science, and Technical Subjects* (2010).

Reading: Literature and Informational Text

Does the child . . .

✓ Ask and answer questions about key details in a text? (Grades K–5) See *Before, During, and After*, page 118

✓ Refer to details and examples in a text when answering questions and asking or explaining what the text says? (Grades K–5) See *Stump the Grown Up*, page 132

✓ Recall and retell familiar stories, including key details with or without prompting and support? (Grades K–3) See *Laugh It Up*, page 126

✓ Recount stories, including fables and folktales from diverse cultures, and determine the central message, lesson, or moral? (Grades 2–5) See *Reading is Everywhere*, page 129

✓ Determine a theme of a story, drama, or poem from details in the text? (Grades 4–5) See *Show It When You Know It*, page 131

If you answered "yes" to questions that apply to a child at the grade level(s) identified, this may be an area of strength for the child. If you answered "no," it may be an area that needs support.

Use the grade levels indicated for each strategy to assist in selecting strategies designed to support the children in achieving Kindergarten through Grade 5 expectations identified in Appendix D.

Before, During, and After

Thinking about Meaning

Materials

- story or articles
- notepaper
- pen or pencil

Grade Levels

- Kindergarten
- Grades 1–5

Help your child improve comprehension by taking a few minutes to ask questions before, during, and after reading with your child.

- Ask your child to help you choose a story or article to read.

- Read the passage before your child reads it.

- Think of questions you can ask before, during, and after your child reads.

- Avoid questions that prompt your child to respond with "yes" or "no." Ask questions that encourage your child to predict before reading, think while reading, and draw conclusions after reading.

  - PREDICT BEFORE READING: As you look at the pictures, what do you think this story/article will be about? Why? … Will this be funny, sad, or scary? How do you know? How do you think the character will be the same or different from people you know?

  - THINK WHILE READING: What do you think will happen next? Why do you think that will happen? … How does the picture on this page match what you are reading?

  - DRAW CONCLUSIONS AFTER READING: How did the story compare to what you predicted? … How would you sum up the main events of the story? … What are some things we have done as a family that are the same as the events in this story?

- Ask questions during natural breaks in the story or article to enrich meaning and enhance interest.

- Invite your child to read the story with you again.

As you read again, encourage your child to ASK you questions Before, During, and After reading! (Suggestions: Explore websites listed in Appendix B for Online Book Lists.)

Go and Know
Gaining Background Knowledge

1/2 Day

The more you and your child go, the more your child will know!

PART 1: BEFORE READING

Materials
- books or magazines
- I Know Grid (page 121)

- Ask your child or your child's teacher about topics that will be read about in school in the near future OR choose a favorite subject with your child, such as animals, insects, dinosaurs, or space.

- Ask your child's teacher to suggest books or magazine articles about the subject that you can read with your child. (Also, see Appendix B: Online Book Lists.)

Grade Levels
- Kindergarten
- Grades 1–5

- Look through the books or articles with your child as you ask questions to learn what your child knows about the topic.

- Plan visits to places with your child in person or online that will help build your child's background knowledge about the subject you are reading. For example, if you choose animal books, you might visit a zoo, farm, nature center, or animal shelter. If you choose to read about special cultural events or celebrations, consider visiting events and places in the community representing different cultures.

- During the in-person or online visits, discuss what you and your child observe.

- Invite your child to answer "Before I Read ..." questions on the "I Know Grid" (page 121)—"What do I know about this topic? What do I think the author will share?"

PART 2: DURING READING

- Compare what you read to what you and your child observed during your in-person or online visits.

PART 3: AFTER READING

- Invite your child to answer the questions on the three other parts of the "I Know Grid":

  • After Reading: What are some important facts shared by the author?

  • New Information: What are five or more things I learned from reading or visiting the special places?

  • Future Goals: What do I still want to know about this topic?

Throughout the year, keep copies of the "I Know Grid" you and your child completed to see all that your child learned as you "Go and Know" together.

I Know Grid
(Organizer for reading and writing nonfiction)

My Name: Date: _____

Title: _____

Author: _____ Illustrator: _____

Topic: (Subject area/content): _____

## Before I Read . . . **What do I know about this topic?** **What do I think the author will share?**	## After Reading . . . **What are some important facts shared by the author?**
## New Information . . . **What are five or more things I learned from reading or visiting the special places?** 1. 2. 3. 4. 5.	## Future Goal . . . **What do I still want to know about this topic?**

I Can Read It and Do It!

Understanding a Purpose for Reading

Materials

- set of directions for models
- science experiments
- recipes
- toy assembly or craft projects

Grade Levels

- Grades 3–5

Choose a special project that requires reading two or more sequential directions such as building a model, completing a science experiment, following a recipe, putting together a toy, or making a craft.

- Invite your child to read independently or listen as you read the directions aloud.

- Encourage your child to follow each direction in sequence as it is read.

- Offer help as needed.

- Display the project to show your child and let family members know how proud you are that your child could read it and do it.

It's Fun to Organize

Organizing and Communicating Ideas

Help your child organize ideas and information before and after reading with these few easy steps.

- Invite your child to choose a story, a nonfiction passage, or a poem to read.

BEFORE READING ...

- Before reading, guide your child to choose an organizer to match the type of reading passage that was selected. Use ...

  - "Story Map" for fiction.

  - "I Know Grid" for nonfiction.

  - "Poetry Flower" for poetry.

- Discuss the organizer. What parts should be completed before reading?

READ ...

- Invite your child to read independently or listen as you read.

AFTER READING ...

- Guide your child to complete the organizer.

- Go back, as needed, to the passage to help your child reread sections of the text to find information that will make the organizer as complete as possible.

WRITING ...

- Invite your child to use an organizer before writing to develop a meaningful writing plan.

Materials

- picture book, story, nonfiction article, poem
- "Story Map" for story/fiction on page 124
- "I Know Grid" for nonfiction/ informational text on page 121
- "Poetry Flower" for use with a poem on page 125

Grade Levels

- Kindergarten
- Grades 1–5

Story Map

(Organizer for reading or writing a fictional story)

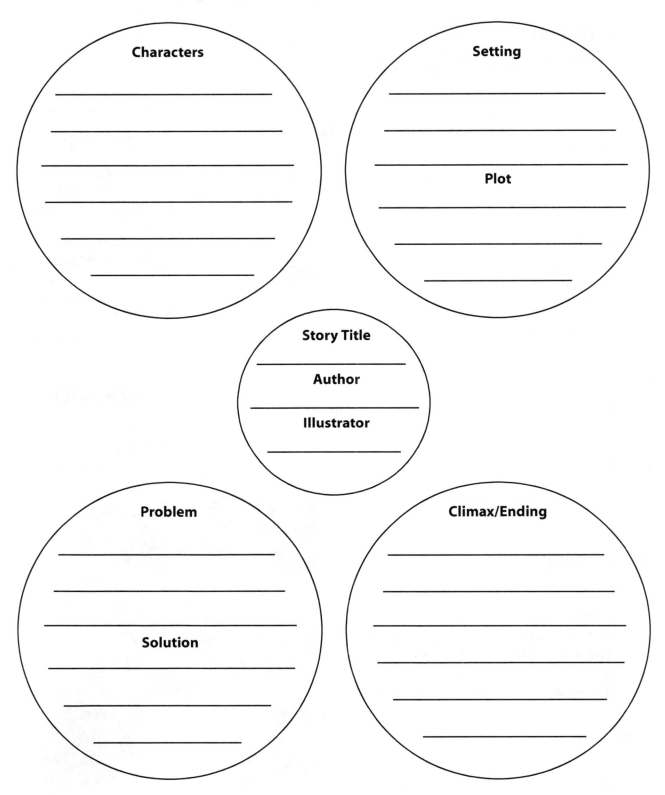

Characters

Setting

Plot

Story Title

Author

Illustrator

Problem

Solution

Climax/Ending

Poetry Flower

(Organizer for Poetry)

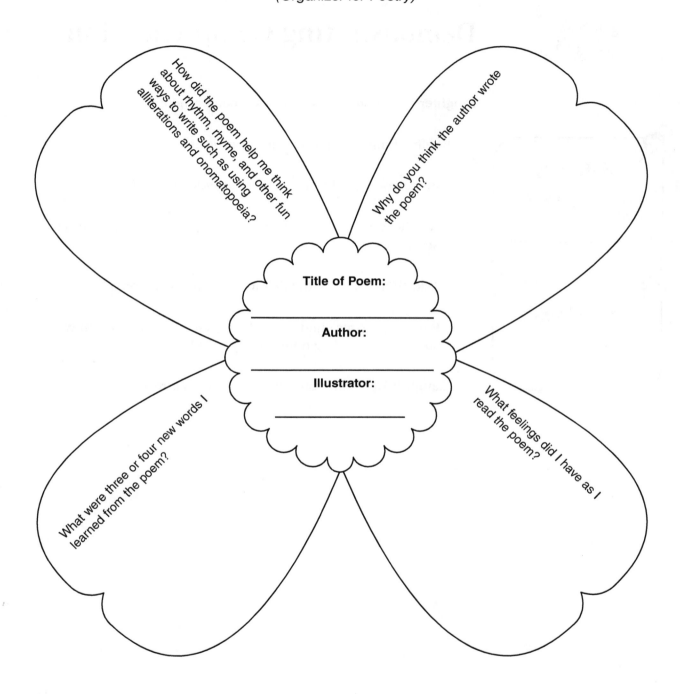

How did the poem help me think about rhythm, rhyme, and other fun ways to write such as using alliterations and onomatopoeia?

Why do you think the author wrote the poem?

Title of Poem:

_____

Author:

_____

Illustrator:

_____

What were three or four new words I learned from the poem?

What feelings did I have as I read the poem?

Laugh It Up
Demonstrating Comprehension

Laughter is a great way to check on comprehension.

Materials
• funny stories, poems, jokes, articles

Grade Levels
• Kindergarten
• Grades 1–5

- Select funny stories, poems, or articles.

- Invite your child to listen or read independently.

- Watch—does your child laugh or smile while reading funny sentences?

- Ask, "What was funny? Tell me in your own words."

- Encourage your child to read and retell the joke or funny story to a friend or other family member.

"Laugh It Up" with your child to show that reading can be fun.

Picture It

Improving Listening Comprehension

It's easy and fun for your child to "Picture It!"

- Read a picture book aloud to your child, but do not show the pictures.

- Encourage your child to visualize what is read. Say, "Make pictures in your mind about what I read to you."

- Invite your child to draw some of the "mind pictures" as you read.

- After you finish reading, invite your child to create other pictures that retell the key points of what was read.

- Read the book again as you show the illustrations to your child. Discuss how your child's pictures included details that were similar to or different from the illustrations in the book.

- Invite your child to retell the story as you share the pictures with other family members and friends.

Materials

- picture book
- paper
- drawing markers/crayons

Grade Levels

- Kindergarten
- Grades 1–5

Positive Role Models

Gaining a Sense of Purpose for Learning

Materials

- books, articles, and videos about highly-respected famous people
- writing paper
- pencil or pen

Grade Levels

- Kindergarten
- Grades 1–5

Favorite and highly-respected sports figures, television and movie stars, and musicians can help your child learn!

- Gather books and articles from magazines or newspapers.

- Select videos about two or three positive role models.

- Read about each famous person with your child.

- Discuss their struggles and triumphs.

- Help your child find addresses for famous people. (Addresses are available through public relations offices or publishers.)

- Invite your child to write and ask for pictures and responses to questions related to challenges they faced when young that you child is experiencing as a student.

Reading is All Around

Developing an Interest in Reading

Fun opportunities for reading and learning are "All Around!" All you have to do is show your child where to look! It's easy.

- Read aloud and discuss magazine and newspaper articles or stories.

- Share recipes while cooking.

- Read advertisements and select "best buys" with your child.

- Share with your child letters and emails from relatives and friends.

- Find ways to connect everyday experiences and your child's interests to reading.

These simple actions show your child that Reading is All Around!

Materials

- real-world reading materials
- magazine and newspaper articles
- stories
- recipes
- advertisements
- letters

Grade Levels

- Kindergarten
- Grades 1–5

Reading Is Everywhere!

Understanding That Reading and Listening Have a Purpose

Materials

- several types of reading materials (magazine articles, music lyrics, recipes, game or toy manuals, birthday cards, letters)

Grade Levels

- Kindergarten
- Grades 1–5

This is as easy as placing a few reading materials around the house.

- Invite your child to name interests and hobbies, such as playing a sport, cooking, or playing an instrument.

- Gather several reading materials about your child's interests.

- Display the material everywhere—in the bathroom, on coffee tables, in the car, on dressers, and on bookshelves.

- Invite your child to read the materials alone or read with your child.

- Discuss the reading material together and with the family.

- Ask your child to retell what was read, using words your child chooses.

- Change the reading samples as your child's interests change.

Show It When You Know It

Showing Understanding

All this activity requires is a good book or article and a little imagination!

- Invite your child to choose a story such as a fairy tale, myth, or fable.

- Preview the story with your child to discuss how it compares to other stories that your child has read or heard.

- Invite your child to read the story, with you or independently.

- Ask your child to retell the story sharing the sequence of events as they happened.

- Guide your child to follow the sequence by asking, "What happened first? What happened next … ?"

- Ask your child, "How do we know this story is fiction or non-fiction?"

- Invite your child to save the memory of the special events in the story by drawing pictures or making a collage of pictures cut from magazines or newspapers.

- Ask your child to write somewhere on the artwork page the title of what was read and a brief description of the picture(s) and how they are a reminder of what was read. Also, add your child's name.

- Display the story memories and encourage your child to share the story and the pictures with others.

Invite your child to retell stories in different ways throughout the year. Date each illustrated story, so you and your child will see the story memories grow.

Materials
- book or article
- writing or drawing supplies
- magazine or advertisement cutouts
- scissors
- glue

Grade Levels
- Kindergarten
- Grades 1–5

Stump the Grown-Up

Asking and Answering Questions

Materials

• story or article

Grade Levels

• Kindergarten
• Grades 1–5

Is turnabout really fair play?

● Read a story or article aloud with your child or invite your child to read to you.

● As you read together, ask your child to think of questions to ask you about the story or article.

● Challenge your child to try to stump you.

● Then, it's your turn.

● Ask your child two or three questions about the reading passage.

● If needed, help your child find the answers in the passage by rereading, using picture clues, or looking through the pages to remember story sequence.

● Take turns asking and answering questions.

Watch out, your child may learn many ways to "Stump the Grown-Up."

Take a Wild Guess

Predicting

Before "digging in" to the story for the first time, invite your child to take a wild guess!

- Invite your child to choose a story that is not familiar, such as a fairy tale, myth, folktale, or fable.

- Before reading, discuss with your child the title and illustration on the cover.

- Discuss the names and roles of author and illustrator.

- Ask your child to guess what the story will be about while looking at the pictures and other clues. (See *Story Map* on page 124.)

- Discuss the characters, setting, and plot, and ask your child to guess what will happen in the story.

- Read the book together.

- Acknowledge your child's correct "guesses" as you read.

- Ask your child how the author's use of characters, plot, and setting may be the same as or different from other authors your child knows who have written on similar topics.

- Remind your child to do the same when reading alone.

When your child guesses and makes predictions before and during a reading selection, less time is spent figuring out meaning after reading.

Materials
- fictional story
- Story Map (page 124)

Grade Levels
- Kindergarten
- Grades 1–5

Writing

Each year in their writing, students should demonstrate increasing sophistication in all aspects of language use, from vocabulary and syntax to the development and organization of ideas, and they should address increasing demanding content and sources.

Source: National Governors Association Center for Best Practices, Council of Chief State School Officers (2010) *Common Core State Standards for English Language Arts & Literacy in History/Social Studies, Science, and Technical Subjects* (2010) p. 19

Consider the following questions as you observe children in K–Grade 5 to determine which of the following *Writing* strategies can build on a child's literacy strengths and which strategies can support areas of greatest need.

The questions below are adapted from the K–5 *Common Core State Standards for English Language Arts & Literacy in History/Social Studies, Science, and Technical Subjects* (2010).

Writing

Does the child . . .

✓ Print uppercase and lowercase letters correctly? (K–Grade 1) See *Turn It Around*, page 155

✓ Use a combination of drawing, dictating, and writing and other text features to compose informative texts? (Kindergarten–Grade 2) See *Create a Caption*, page 139

✓ Recall information from experiences to answer questions and write responses? (K–Grade 5) See *Why Read and Write?*, page 156

✓ Write informative texts in which the child names a topic and provides some facts about the topic? (Grades 1–5) See *Be on the Lookout*, page 137

✓ Write opinion pieces on topics or texts, supporting a point of view with reasons? (Grades 1–5) See *Be On the Lookout*, page 137

✓ With guidance and support from adults, respond to questions and suggestions from peers and add details to strengthen writing as needed? (K–Grade 5) See *Good-Work Meeting Day*, page 141

✓ Explore a variety of digital tools to produce and publish writing? (K–Grade 5) See *Letter-Message Guide*, page 144

If you answered "yes" to questions that apply to a child at the grade level(s) identified, this may be an area of strength for the child. If you answered "no," it may be an area that needs support.

Use the grade levels indicated for each strategy to assist in selecting strategies designed to support the children in achieving Kindergarten through Grade 5 expectations identified in Appendix D.

A Special Place
Writing Comfortably

Anytime

Choose a special place that can best support your child's writing performance.

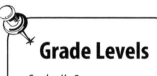

Materials

- table or desk
- comfortable chair
- good lighting
- writing materials (pens, pencils, markers, crayons, paper)

Grade Levels

- Grades K–5

- Invite your child to help choose a writing space in a quiet corner or out-of-the-way room with a table or desk, a comfortable chair, good lighting, and writing materials such as pens, pencils, markers, crayons, and a variety of paper.

- Choose a place where letters and correctly-spelled words can be displayed as helpful reminders to use when writing. For example:

    1. Uppercase and lowercase letters in alphabetical order using the same form being taught at school.

    2. Grade-appropriate high-frequency words in alphabetical order such as *said, says, was, were, what, who, why.*

    3. Words from special topics listed alphabetically and grouped in themes (holidays, seasons, sports, foods, etc.)

- Encourage your child to write in this special place and refer to the letters and words, as needed.

Be on the Lookout

Gaining Writing Skills by Writing Frequently

Be on the lookout for everyday, meaningful opportunities for your child to write!

Materials
• writing paper
• pencil or pen

• Writing could include diary entries, grocery lists, holiday and birthday cards, telephone messages, notes to friends, trip planning, thank-you notes, or party invitations. No writing task is too small. Each gives excellent practice!

Grade Levels
• Kindergarten
• Grades 1–5

• Encourage your child to write about something that was recently experienced, read, or heard.

• Ask your child to share an opinion or preference about what was experienced or what was in a book.

• Be patient if your child seems hesitant to write. There may be times when writing interest is high and other times when interest is low.

• Young children should be given the option to share by drawing, dictating, or writing.

• Keep watching, keep offering, and keep encouraging. Soon your child will choose to write spontaneously without being asked to write.

Break It Up

Setting Goals and Completing Complex Assignments

Materials

- school assignment
- writing paper
- pencil or pen

Grade Levels

- Kindergarten
- Grades 1–5

Breaking up is easy to do with this sensible activity!

- Help your child manage a complex school assignment by breaking it up into a sequence of individual steps … or "chunks."

- Discuss the steps necessary to complete the assignment successfully.

- Ask questions such as, "How will you know when you are finished?" "What do you have to do to get to the 'finish line'?"

- Ask your child to name each step necessary to finish the assignment.

- List the steps in writing (and modify them, as necessary) while your child completes the assignment.

- Congratulate your child as each step is completed.

Create a Caption

Writing Descriptive Words and Phrases

60 minutes

Remember special times by giving your child a little writing practice with this fun activity!

- Invite your child to create a scrapbook or photo album for a special family event.

- Give your child copies of photos from the event to put in the scrapbook or photo album.

- Ask your child to write or dictate as you write captions next to the photos.

- For extra fun, attach dialogue-filled "speech bubbles" to the photos to show what a person in the picture may be saying.

- Invite your child to finish the pages with stickers, rubber stamps, or paper cutouts that reflect the primary purpose of the event (birthday, holiday, vacation, etc.).

Display the album in a special place to share with family and friends.

Materials

- photographs
- scrapbook or photo album
- writing paper
- scissors
- tape or photo adhesive
- page decorations (stickers, rubber stamps, paper cutouts)

Grade Levels

- Kindergarten
- Grades 1–2

Gifts for Writing Fun!

Writing about Everyday Experiences

Give the gift that lasts a lifetime ... the gift of writing!

● Encourage your child to write by talking with your child about fun writing gifts she/he would like and might also give as a gift to a friend. Suggest a variety of pens and pencils, pads of paper, stationery, envelopes, or a notebook for a diary or daily journal.

● Special gifts can also include books, computer software, a dictionary, thesaurus, or an almanac. Show your child how to use them as you model writing about special experiences and including dates next to each entry.

● Your time together will be fun and well spent!

Good-Work Meeting Day
Emphasizing Strengths

Have a "Good-Work Meeting Day" and watch your child's self-esteem and learning grow!

PREPARE FOR THE MEETING ...

- Use a special container for your child's completed schoolwork. For example, label a special "Homework Box."

- Invite your child to place completed work that the teacher has reviewed in the container.

- Designate a special day each week or each month as "Good-Work Meeting Day."

- Before meeting with your child, go through the schoolwork.

- Choose one sample of good work to help you work together to set a "Stress a Strength" goal.

- Choose one piece of work that was challenging to set a "Nurture a Need" goal.

Materials
- container for schoolwork
- schoolwork samples

Grade Levels
- Kindergarten
- Grades 1–5

MEETING TIME!

- Without showing the pieces of homework you have chosen, invite your child to briefly review the work in the container, and then select two pieces in the same manner you did. (One piece that your child selects as a "strength" and one as a "need".)

- During the meeting, discuss the samples that were chosen by you and your child.

- Encourage your child to ask questions about your selections.

- Write or illustrate by drawing a list of strength and need goals at each meeting using the selected work as a guide. Examples: Strength Goal—*I will keep writing neatly so others can read what I write.* Needs Goal—*I will think carefully before I write, so my ideas are in complete sentences that begin with an uppercase letter and end with the correct punctuation.*

Keep a notebook or file box organized chronologically or by subject area to show how your child's goals have been met over time.

Less May Be Best

Adjust Assignments to Reach Learning Goals

Take the "Less May Be Best" approach by encouraging your child to reflect on work habits when completing school assignments. Assignments related to one skill, such as learning to spell words or recalling story sequence, will help focus the reflections so that you and your child can communicate about setting future goals.

JOURNAL RECORD . . .

- Ask your child to briefly record in a journal or notebook the date and title of an important assignment.

- Record how long it took to complete an assignment and how easy or challenging the assignment appeared to be.

- Add notes to your child's journal entries describing the behaviors you observed while the assignment was being completed (questions asked, signs of independence or frustration, etc.).

- Discuss your observations with your child.

- If your child's reflections and your observations indicate that your child is experiencing a great deal of frustration and needing your consistent help in completing the assignments, suggest that you request a parent-student-teacher conference.

Materials

- notebook/journal
- pen/pencil

Grade Levels

- Kindergarten
- Grades 1–5

SHARE WITH THE TEACHER...

- Call the teacher to request an appointment for a parent-student-teacher conference where you both can share journal entries with samples of your child's work.

- Encourage your child to clearly and respectfully describe to the teacher the behaviors and experiences you both recorded in the journal.

- Ask the teacher for suggestions about adjusting the assignment, so your child can produce the best results.

- For many children, "Less May Be Best" when learning new skills. Ask the teacher if your child can do less on an assignment, so the best that your child can do is shown in what is completed.

Changes may need to be made at home and school to adjust assignments to help your child learn more and achieve realistic goals.

Letter-Message Guide

Becoming an Independent Message-Writer

Materials

- paper or digital device to write a letter
- pencil or pen

Grade Levels

- Kindergarten
- Grades 1–5

Use a "Letter-Message Guide" to support your child's letter/message-writing independence. Encourage writing to different audiences by writing a letter on paper or keyboarding on a digital device.

Point out the importance of the date, salutation or greeting, body of the message, closing, and signature or printed name when typing the message.

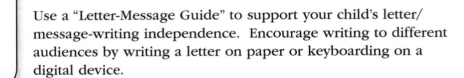

Date: Enter dates on handwritten letters. Dates are not usually needed on digital messages, because dates are recorded on most digital devices.

| Salutation or Greeting | _____ |

Dear _____,

Body/Message	_____
	_____
	_____
	_____

Closing (For example, "Love, Sincerely, …")

Name of Sender: Write name on paper message. Type name on digital device.

Love ,

_____

My Daily Schedule

Taking Responsibility for Daily Activities

It's not how much your child needs to do each day, it's how well your child can take responsibility for what to do daily.

Materials

- display board or large piece of paper or card stock
- pencil/pen or markers
- Optional: binder clips next to each item on the schedule

- Talk with your child about how your daily schedule on Mondays through Fridays differs from what you do on the weekends.

- Ask your child how her/his Monday through Friday schedule during the school year looks like compared to weekends.

- Did your child mention meals, school, play, and study/homework times on Mondays through Fridays during the school year?

Grade Levels

- Grades K–5

- Invite your child to discuss with you and then write a weekday schedule on a display board or large piece of paper or card stock. Put it where it can be seen easily each day.

- Ask your child to suggest times for some activities such as playtimes and study times.

- For example, your child may choose to study immediately after school, just before dinner, or after dinner.

- Optional: Clip a binder clip next to each item on the schedule. Ask your child to flip the clip to activities as they are completed each day.

- When the study schedule and other activities are planned and posted where others can see, the question becomes, "When did you choose to play or study?" rather than, "When did I tell you that you should study or you can play?"

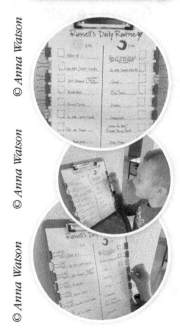

© Anna Watson

Our daughter and 6-year-old grandson created this daily schedule. As Russell finishes something on the list, he flips the clip toward the list.

No Boundaries

Exploring Letters and Words

Materials

- The Alphabet in Print chart (page 96)
- unlined paper
- pencils of different sizes
- file folder
- different sizes and colors of crayons

Grade Levels

- Kindergarten
- Grade 1

DRAW ...

- Invite your child to talk with you about a memory of a special experience or about plans for an upcoming event. Ask your child to draw a picture about the experience or event on unlined paper.

- Discuss words that describe the picture.

WRITE ...

- Invite your child to explore writing the words on the unlined paper. Focus on the form of the letters ... and **not on perfect spelling**.

- Encourage your child to refer to The Alphabet in Print chart on page 96 to help.

OBSERVE ...

- Watch your child write.

  - Is the pencil or crayon being held correctly and comfortably?

  - What size pencil most comfortably supports your child's best writing?

  - Are the letters and words being written from left to right?

  - Are the letters spaced carefully within the words?

- Write the date on each drawing with a brief description of what you saw your child do as you observed.

HELP ...

- Offer help in forming the letters, as needed.

Save samples and notes in a file folder as a record of how your child is growing as a writer.

Notice the "Good Stuff"

Becoming a Willing, Confident Writer

This one's easy. All you have to do is notice the "good stuff."

● Whenever you can, acknowledge your child's writing, looking for what is most appropriate for your child's age and grade level.

● Focus on letter and word formation, content, spelling, and punctuation and/or grammar, as appropriate for your child's age and grade.

● Emphasize your child's writing successes by using phrases that reflect what the teacher suggested or provided in a rubric or scoring guide that shows what was expected at your child's age and grade. For example:

  • *The words you chose and wrote are clearly written, so others can read what you wrote.*

  • *The first paragraph is clear and gives a clear idea of what you plan to share in your report.*

  • *You clearly describe the setting and the characters in the story.*

  • *The events in your summary are in logical order.*

  • *I can see that you checked your spelling.*

When you notice the "good stuff," it will keep happening!

Perfect Pen Pals

Writing for a Purpose

Materials

- notes, letters, and email from relatives and friends
- writing paper or computer
- envelopes, stamps

Grade Levels

- Kindergarten
- Grades 1–5

Help your child stay in touch with friends and family members who can make "Perfect Pen Pals."

- Ask a friend or relative to write a note, letter, or email to your child.

- Encourage your child to respond.

- Copy the Letter-Message Guide from page 144 to help your child write a letter using the correct form.

- Help address envelopes, as needed, or guide your child to write email messages.

- Keep the communication going.

Your child will become a better writer and could have pen pals for years to come!

Playing Secretary

Connecting Spoken Language to Writing

Enjoy a "Writing Conversation" by "playing secretary" as your child shares experiences and watches as someone puts the child's spoken words into print. Play secretary to help your child communicate and see spoken words transformed into print at home or anywhere.

- Talk about a recent experience with your child. (For example, share photos from a recent family trip or discuss a special event.)

- Say, "Please tell me in one or two sentences what you want to remember about this experience."

- On a piece of paper, write your child's response word-for-word. (Do not change words when writing the first draft.)

- Read the response aloud to your child. Then, invite your child to have a "Writing Conversation." Ask questions such as, "Are your ideas in complete sentences, so others can enjoy them?" (If basic grammar changes are needed, suggest changes, so "the words and sentences sound like language we would read in a book.") Make the changes in Draft 2.

- Occasionally, ask your child to copy the changes that you wrote in Draft 2.

- Invite your child to read and draw an illustration for Draft 2 or glue copies of photos that are reminders of the experience.

- Date and display your child's work.

- Keep copies to see reading and writing grow.

The stories your child dictates and illustrates after the "Writing Conversation" will become a treasure of memories to keep.

Materials

- writing and drawing paper or photos
- crayons/markers
- camera (optional)

Grade Levels

- Kindergarten
- Grades 1–4

See Writing Grow

Writing Smoothly and Confidently

Materials

- reading material that gives reader strong feelings
- writing paper
- clock
- pencil or pen
- file folder

Grade Levels

- Kindergarten
- Grades 1–5

Reading and writing go together and can grow together.

READ...

- Invite your child to help choose a story or article that prompts a sense of emotion (happiness, sadness, anger, etc.).
- Invite your child to read it independently or aloud with you.

WRITE...

- Ask your child to share by drawing or writing special thoughts and feelings from reading the passage.
- Encourage your child to draw and write as much as possible for five minutes without taking a break to check on spelling or punctuation.
- The goal is to communicate ideas and feelings. There should be no pressure to write perfectly.
- You may help your child focus with an encouraging word or by your presence—sitting next to your child while writing.
- After five minutes, invite your child to read and/or use the illustrations to retell what is written.

DISCUSS...

- Discuss the ideas that were written and/or drawn.
- Write the date on the writing or illustration and save the work in a "first draft" file folder.
- After a short time on the same day or on another day, take the first draft out of the folder. Ask your child to read what was written and/or illustrated in the first draft.
- Write Draft 2 on another paper. Use print or cursive with correct spelling to show your child what can be written in the final version.

- Ask your child to read what you wrote and write the Final Copy below what you wrote or on a separate paper.

- If the work is to be given to the teacher, ask your child and the teacher for guidance.

  - Should the first draft be handed in with a final copy?

  - What process should be followed to edit or update the work to continually improve your child's writing?

  - Does the teacher have a scoring guide to follow in guiding your child's writing in the future?

Watch writing grow over time, and you can support your child's writing growth by giving guidance that supports classroom goals.

Sloppy Copy

Gaining Confidence Forming Letters, Words, and Sentences

Materials

- writing paper
- pencil or pen

Grade Levels

- Kindergarten
- Grades 1–5

Your child will be able to concentrate on ideas first when encouraged to write a "sloppy copy" before writing a "good copy."

- Encourage your child to plan to make more than one copy when writing, whether it is a short thank-you note, story, or report.

- Explain that the first copy (sloppy copy) is to practice getting ideas on paper.

- Do not stop your child to make instant corrections.

- Watch for signals that your child needs help. Are there frequent erasures, spelling questions, long pauses between writing?

- Encourage your child with a gentle reminder that the sloppy copy is to get the ideas down first.

- Read aloud and discuss the sloppy copy.

- Edit it with your child by correcting spelling, punctuation, and any wording that will help make ideas clearer.

- Invite your child to copy the new version with the corrections on a different piece of paper.

- Comment as your child writes to guide her/him to form the letters and words carefully while improving spelling, grammar, and punctuation.

Use Sloppy Copy to help your child gain writing practice and grow as a writer.

The Writing Process

Seeing Writing as a Journey

Does your child have a school assignment that will be displayed and should be "just right"? Use the writing process to help complete the assignment and support your child's growth as a writer. Your child may not need to follow the process when writing lists, short notes, stories just for fun, or journal entries. Discuss each step before writing begins.

The Process

1. Invite your child to think about ideas that can be shared in writing. (Organizers such as the Story Map and Poetry Flower on pages 124 and 125 can help prepare for writing.)

2. Ask guiding questions to help your child think about the ideas in a logical order.

3. Guide your child to use a rubric or scoring guide provided by your child's teacher when writing.

4. Offer guidance to help your child address the expectations outlined in the rubric.

5. Note strong points that make ideas clear and understandable for people who are reading what was written. What evidence shows that the expectations on the rubric were met?

6. Follow the teacher's guidelines as you edit and revise the first draft *with* your child (not *for* your child) to correct spelling, grammar, punctuation, and meet other expectations for clarity. Show your child how important it is to proofread.

7. Ask your child to write a final draft using the best handwriting ... or using a word processing program.

8. Invite your child to write a title page, design a cover, and prepare illustrations.

Materials

- writing paper
- construction/drawing paper
- markers
- crayons
- computer
- writing rubric or scoring guide from teacher

Grade Levels

- Kindergarten
- Grades 1–5

To-Do Lists

Discussing and Recording Commitments

Materials

- notebook, calendar, formal assignment notebook, or display board

Grade Levels

- Kindergarten
- Grades 1–5

"To-do" lists aren't just for grown-ups. Your child can benefit from them, too.

- Help your child pick out a special organizer such as a notebook, calendar, formal assignment book, or display board.

- Invite your child to list or illustrate a reasonable, age-appropriate number of specific to-do goals each day or each week. For example, list visits to special places or food shopping for a special gathering of friends.

- Ask your child to dictate, write, or draw the list to display for all to see.

- Count the number of items on the list. Try to limit the number of items per week to a maximum number equal to your child's age.

- At the end of the day or end of the week, invite your child to identify the number of goals achieved. Discuss how important the other goals are and how they can best be achieved.

- Invite your child to update the list regularly.

Congratulate your child for all the jobs completed!

Cindy's To-do List
1. Clean Room.
2. Practice piano ___ minutes each day.
   ... out with sister.
   ... ead for 20 minutes.
5. Study Spelling.

Turn It Around

Forming Letters, Numbers, and Words Correctly

30 minutes

Never fear; reversing letters, numbers, and words is a normal part of learning to read and write. Common letter and number reversals are *d* and *b*, *p* and *q*, *3* and *5*, *6* and *9*. Reversals can be letters or words written from right to left or upside down.

- Keep a list of reversals your child consistently makes when writing.

- Write the letters as part of words such as *cab, bed, man*.

- Share helpful reminders such as the "b" and "d" look at each other in "bed."

- Draw pictures next to the words, so your child can associate the sound made by the letter within the word.

- Display the highlighted words with the pictures where your child can see them while writing.

- Invite your child to look at the letter/picture chart while writing to see how letters in words are formed.

- If your child consistently reverses letters and/or words, talk with your child's teacher. Ask how you can support your child by using methods the teacher is using to help your child learn to write the letters and words correctly.

Your child's teacher will be able to offer other suggestions. Consider trying "Rainbow Word Trace-Over" (page 107) and "At Close Range" (page 93) as other ways to help your child with reversals.

Materials
- writing paper
- construction or drawing paper
- tape
- pen or pencil

Grade Levels
- Kindergarten
- Grade 1

Why Read and Write?

Connecting the Real World to Learning at School

Help your child answer the question "Why is it important to learn to read and write?"

- Select a story, a book, or an article about people in different jobs and careers (scientists, teachers, police officers, military, fire fighters, mathematicians, sales people …)

- Dicuss different jobs family members currently are working or have experienced in the past.

- Discuss each job as you read and complete the "Why Read and Write?" chart together.

As you complete each section of the chart, ask your child, "Why is it important to learn to read and write?"

Why Read and Write?

Career or Job	One way a person in that job uses reading and writing.	How can I learn the same reading and writing skills?
1.		
2.		
3.		

Write Away

Writing for a Variety of Purposes

Materials

- magazines
- cereal boxes
- newspapers
- letter-message guide (page 143)
- envelopes
- stamps
- optional: computer with email access

Grade Levels

- Grades 3–5

Get out the postage stamps. Your child won't want to stop writing after writing a letter and receiving something in return.

- Encourage your child to read magazines, cereal boxes, and newspapers to find addresses for information packets, free samples, travel brochures, or anything that is free.

- Show your child how to write letters or email messages to ask for items and information.

- Demonstrate for your child how to write a letter with the date, greeting, message, and closing signature or an email with greeting and message.

- Encourage your child to write a first draft and follow the Writing Process described on page 153.

- If your child is sending a letter, help stamp, address, and mail the envelope with the letter.

- When writing an email message, guide your child through the process.

Writing will have so much more meaning when your child sees real results from hard work!

"Write On"
Gaining Purpose and a Clear Plan for Writing

Encourage your child to "write on" by asking the most applicable writer's guide questions. Ask the questions as you guide your child through the "Writing Process" (page 153).

Writer's Guide

1. Ideas
- Why are you writing this?
- Who will read what you write?
- Do you plan to display or publish your writing?
- What expectations does your teacher have?
- What guidelines does the rubric (or scoring guide) offer you?
- What do you need to know to write what is expected?
- When will writing begin, and when do you need to be finished?

2. Organization
- Do you have a clear writing plan?
- What will you use to organize, save, and keep track of your writing?

3. Drafts: Edit and Revise
- Are your ideas understandable?
- Do your ideas flow naturally and make sense together?
- Have you carefully checked for correct spelling, punctuation, and other expectations?
- What can you do to make your writing clear, fluent, and meaningful with correct grammar?

4. Discuss
- Does your teacher want to see the first draft?
- How does your writing show that you are communicating to your intended audience?
- What have you done to make your writing clear and meaningful?

5. Revision
- What changes are still needed to do your best work?

6. Final Draft
- Have you used your best handwriting or word processing skills?

7. Presentation
- How will you "show off" your final draft in an attractive, interesting way?

Materials
- writing paper
- pencil/pen

Grade Levels
- Kindergarten
- Grades 1–5

Appendix A
References and Family Literacy Resources

Appendix A includes references for quotes cited in *Family Time Reading Fun* and books and articles recommended as family literacy resources.

Beck, Isabel L., McKeown, M. G., & Kucan, L. (2013). *Bringing words to life: Robust vocabulary instruction.* 2nd ed. New York, NY: The Guilford Press.

California Department of Education. (2008). *California Preschool Learning Foundations* (Vol. 1). Sacramento, CA. (http://www.cde.ca.gov/sp/cd/re/documents/preschoollf.pdf)

California Department of Education. (2010). *California Preschool Learning Foundations* (Vol. 2) Sacramento. https://www.cde.ca.gov/sp/cd/re/documents/preschoolfoundationsvol3.pdf

California State University Center for the Advancement of Reading. (2019). *The early years: Promoting a promising start in literacy development.* Long Beach, CA: California State University. https://www2.calstate.edu/CAR/Documents/The%20Early%20Years.pdf

Clark, C. (2007). Why it is important to involve parents in their children's literacy development. National Literacy Trust: United Kingdom

Coen, M. T. (2014) *Formative Assessments: What, Why, and How KDP New Teacher Advocate* https://epdf.pub/approaching-difficulties-in-literacy-development-assessment-pedagogy-and-program.html

College of Optometrists in Vision Development (2008). *A Summary of Research and Clinical Studies on Vision and Learning.* https://www.semanticscholar.org/paper/A-SUMMARY-OF-RESEARCH-AND-CLINICAL-STUDIES-ON-AND-Louis/7134f07c2f6f5755a1aaec51f566a53c241d38a0

Connor, C. M. (Ed.) (2016). *The Cognitive Development of Reading and Reading Comprehension.* New York: Routledge

Copple, C., & Bredekamp, S. (2009). *Developmentally appropriate practice in early childhood program-Serving children from birth through age 8.* Washington, DC: National Association for the Education of Young Children.

Cunningham, P.M., & Allington, R. L. (2011). *Classrooms that work: They can all read and write.* (5th ed.). Boston, MA: Allyn and Bacon.

Dickinson, D. K., Morse, A. B. (2019). *Connecting Through Talk: Nurturing Children's Development With Language.* Baltimore, MD: Brookes Publishing

Dunsmore, K., & Fisher D. *Bringing literacy home.* Newark, DE: International Reading Association.

Fletcher-Campbell, F., Reid, G., & Soler, M. (2009). *Approaching difficulties in literacy development: Assessment, pedagogy and programmes.* United Kingdom: The Open University.

Foy, J., & Mann, V. (2003). Home literacy environment and phonological awareness in preschool children: Differential effects for rhyme and phoneme awareness. *Psycholinguistics, 24,* 49-88.

Gentry, R. J. (1996). *My kid can't spell.* Portsmouth. N.H.: Heinemann.

Guthrie, J., & Wigfield, A. (2000). Engagement and motivation in reading. In M. Kamil & P. Mosenthal, D. Pearson, & R. Barr (Eds.), *Handbook of reading research.* Mahwah, N.J.: Earlbaum. 49(7), 518-533.

Haapala, E.A., Eloranta, A., Venäläinen, T. *et al.* Diet quality and academic achievement: a prospective study among primary school children. *European Journal of Nutrition* 56, 2299–2308 (2017). https://doi.org/10.1007/s00394-016-1270-5

Harms, T.; R. Clifford; and D. Cryer. (2005). *Early Childhood Environment Rating Scale,* (Revised edition). New York: Teachers College Pr

Henderson, A. T., & Mapp, K. L. (2002). *New wave of evidence: The impact of school, family, and community connections on student achievement.* Austin, TX.

Howes, C., Downer, J., Pianta, R. (2011) *Dual Language Learners in the Early Childhood Classroom.* Baltimore, MD: Brookes Publishing

Howen, S., Visser, L., Van der Putten, A., Vlaskamp, C. (2016). *The interrelationships between motor, cognitive, and language development in children with and without intellectual and developmental disabilities. Research in Developmental Disabilities.* Amsterdam: Elsevier https://www.sciencedirect.

com/science/article/abs/pii/
S0891422216300129?via%3Dihub

Howes, C., Downer, J., Pianta, R. (2011). *Dual Language Learners in the Early Childhood Classroom.* Baltimore, MD: Brookes Publishing

Juel, C. (1991). Beginning reading. In R. Barr, M. L. Kamil, P. B. Mosenthal, & P. D. Pearson (Eds.), *Handbook of reading research* (pp. 759–788). New York: Longman

Montgomery, J. K. (2019). *The bridge of vocabulary.* 2nd ed. Minneapolis, MN: Pearson.

National Association for the Education of Young Children. (2007). *Promoting positive outcomes for children with disabilities: Recommendations for curriculum, assessment, and program evaluation.* www.naeyc.org/files/naeyc/file/positions/ PrmtgPositiveOutcomes.pdf

National Governors Association Center for Best Practices, Council of Chief State School Officers (2010). *Common Core State Standards for English Language Arts & Literacy in History/Social Studies, Science, and Technical Subjects* National Governors Association Center for Best Practices, Council of Chief State School Officers: Washington D.C. http://www.corestandards.org/ELA-Literacy/

Neuman, S. B., & Dickinson, D. K. (Eds.). (2011). *Handbook of early literacy research* (Vol. 3). New York, NY: The Guilford Press.

North Carolina Foundations Task Force. (2013). *North Carolina foundations for early learning and development.* Raleigh: https://ncchildcare.ncdhhs.gov/ Portals/0/documents/pdf/N/NC_Foundations.pdf

Padak, N., Rasinskik, T. (2005). *Fast Start for Early Readers.* New York: Scholastic

Pressley, M. (2006). *Reading instruction that works: The case for balanced teaching.* New York, NY: The Guilford Press.

Rasinski, T. (2011 K-1, 2008 Gr. 1–2, 2005 Gr. 2–3 & Gr. 4-6), *Daily Word Ladders.* New York: Scholastic. Also see, Also see: https://www.timrasinski.com/

Rasinski, T., Padak, N. (2008). *Fast Start Getting Ready to Read.* New York: Scholastic

Rasinski, T., Smith, M. C. (2019). *Daily Word Ladders: Content Areas Gr. 4+.* New York: Scholastic

Snow, C. E. Burns, S. M. & Griffin P. (Eds.) (1998) *Preventing Reading Difficulties in Young Children.* Washington, D.C.: National Research Council/ National Academy Press

Son, S. H. M., Meisel, S. J. (2006). The Relationship of Young Children's Motor Skills to Later Reading and Math Achievement. *Merrill-Palmer Quarterly, Vol. 52, 755–78.* Detroit: Wayne State University Press

Stanovich, K. E. (1986). Matthew effects in reading: Some consequences of individual differences in the acquisition of literacy. *Reading Research Quarterly, 21.*

Strickland, D.S., Ganske, K., & Monroe, J. K. (2002). *Supporting struggling readers and writers: Strategies for classroom intervention 3-6.* Portland, ME: Stenhouse.

Tabors, P. O. (2008). *One child, two languages.* Baltimore, MD: Brookes.

Worthy, J. & McKool, S. (1996). Students who say they hate to read: The importance of opportunity, choice, and access. In D.J. Leu, C.K. Kinzer, & K.A. Hinchman (Eds.), *Literacies for the 21st century: Research and practice.* 45th yearbook of the National Reading Conference (pp. 245–256). Chicago: National Reading Conference

Yopp, R. H. & Yopp, H. K. (2014). *Literature-Based Reading Activities.* (6th ed.) Boston: Pearson/Allyn & Bacon.

Zero to Three (2010). *Supporting Language and Literacy Skills from 0–12 months,* https://www.zerotothree.org/ resources/1281-supporting-language-and-literacy- skills-from-0-12-months

Appendix B

Online Resources for Parents and Teachers

1. ONLINE FAMILY LITERACY RESOURCES

American Library Association: Association for Library Service to Children
An organization committed to providing exemplary library service to children, their families, and others who work with children.
50 E. Huron
Chicago, IL 60611
Phone Toll Free: 1-800-545-2433
E-mail: alsc@ala.org
Internet address: http://www.ala.org/alsc/
"Great Web Sites for Kids" (http://www.ala.org/great-sites) suggests links to web sites in various categories such as animals, the arts, history & biography, literature & languages, mathematics & computers, sciences, and social sciences

American Speech-Language Hearing Association
Advocate for people with communication disorders.
2200 Research Blvd.
Rockville, Maryland 20850
Members: 800-498-2071
Non-Member: 800-638-8255
Internet address: http://www.asha.org

The Barbara Bush Foundation for Family Literacy
Mission: Establish literacy as a value in every family in America, by helping every family in the nation understand that the home is the child's first school.
P.O. Box 14380
Washington, DC 20044
Phone: 850-562-5300
Internet address: http://www.barbarabush.org

Center for Early Literacy Learning
The goal of the Center for Early Literacy Learning (CELL) is to promote the adoption and sustained use of evidence-based early literacy learning practices. This site has resources for early childhood intervention practitioners, parents, and other caregivers of children, birth to five years of age, with identified disabilities, develop-

mental delays, and those at-risk for poor outcomes. This is an online resource with multiple resources.
Internet address: http://www.earlyliteracylearning.org

Center for Parent Information & Resources
All the materials found on the CPIR Hub have been created and archived for Parent Centers around the country to help them provide support and services to the families they serve.
35 Halsey St., 4th Floor
Newark, NJ 07102
Phone: (973) 642-8100
Internet address: https://www.parentcenterhub.org/

Council for Exceptional Children
Dedicated to improving educational outcomes for individuals with special needs, students with disabilities, and/or the gifted.
3100 Clarendon Blvd, Suite 600 Arlington, VA 22201-5332
Phone: 888-232-7733
Internet address: http://www.cec.sped.org

Family Reading Partnership
A nonprofit community organization that promotes early literacy and provides books and encouragement for families to make reading aloud to their children a part of everyday life.
54 Gunderman Rd.
Ithaca, New York
Phone: 607-277-8602
Email: office@familyreading.org
Internet address: http://www.familyreading.org/

The International Dyslexia Association
A nonprofit organization dedicated to helping individuals with dyslexia, their families and the communities that support them.
40 York Rd. 4th Floor
Baltimore, Maryland 21204
Phone: (410) 296-0232
Fax: (410) 321-5069
Internet address: http://www.interdys.org/

International Literacy Association
Founded as the International Reading Association (IRA), the International Literacy Association (ILA) has worked to enhance literacy instruction through research and professional development for more than 60 years.
P.O. Box 8139 Newark, DE 19714-8139
Phone: 1-800-336-7323 (U.S. and Canada)
302.731.1600 (all other countries)
Internet Address: https://www.literacyworldwide.org

Library of Congress
Children's Literature Center
The Children's Literature Center assists users in gaining access to all children's materials dispersed throughout the Library. The Library holds between 500,000 and 600,000 children's books and periodicals including maps, visual and audio media and secondary material.
101 Independence Ave. SE
Thomas Jefferson Building, LJ 129
Washington, DC 20540-4620
Phone: (202) 707-5535
Internet address: http://www.loc.gov/rr/child/

Literacy Assistance Center
A nonprofit organization dedicated to strengthening and expanding the adult education system, and to advancing adult literacy as a core value in our society and a foundation for equal opportunity and social justice.
85 Broadway Street - 27th Floor
New York, NY 1004
Phone 212-803-3316
Internet address: http://www.lacnyc.org/

National Association of Early Childhood Educators NAEYC For Families
Find research-based resources, tips and ideas for families—from child development to reading, writing, music, math, and more!
NAEYC P.O. Box 97156
Washington, DC 20090-7156
Phone Toll Free: 1-800-424-2460
Phone: 202-232-8777
Internet addresses: http://www.naeyc.org
Information for Families: http://www.naeyc.org/families/

National Center for Family and Community Connections with Schools
Part of Southwest Educational Development Laboratory—Links people with research-based information and resources they can use to effectively connect schools, families, and communities.
4700 Mueller Blvd.
Austin, Texas 78728
Phone Toll Free: 1-800-476-6861
Phone: 202-232-8777

Fax: (512)-476-2286
Internet address: http://www.sedl.org/connections/

National Center for Family Literacy
NCFL works to eradicate poverty through education solutions for families. Partnering with educators, literacy advocates, and policymakers, NCFL develops and provides programming, professional development, and resources that empower and raise families to achieve their potential.
325 West Main Street, Suite 300
Louisville, KY 40202-4237
Phone: 502-584-1133
Internet address: http://www.famlit.org

National Council of Teachers of English
Works to advance teaching, research, and student achievement in English language arts at all levels.
1111 W. Kenyon Road
Urbana, Illinois 61801-1096
Phone Toll Free: 1-877-369-6283
Internet address: http://www.ncte.org
Resources for parents: https://ncte.org/statement/readtogether/

National Parents and Teachers Association (PTA)
National PTA is devoted to the educational success of children and the promotion of family engagement in schools.
1250 N. Pitt St.
Alexandria, VA 22314
Phone Toll Free: 800-307-4782
Fax: 703-836-0942
Internet address: http://pta.org

The Parent Institute for Quality Education
Since 1987, Parent Institute for Quality Education has been engaging, empowering and transforming families by providing the knowledge and the skills to partner with schools and communities to ensure their children achieve their full potential.
22 West 35th St. Suite 201
National City, CA 91950
Phone: 619-420-4730
Internet address: http://www.piqe.org/

PBS Kids.org
Offers a wide variety of resources for parents and children including music, games, and stories.
Public Broadcasting System
http://pbskids.org
This PBS website suggests ways to develop literacy for children ages 2-8: https://www.pbs.org/parents/learn-grow/all-ages/literacy

Read Write Now!
Activities for Reading and Writing Fun: Developed by national reading experts for use with children birth to Grade 6.
http://www.udel.edu/ETL/RWN/Activities.html

ReadWriteThink
ReadWriteThink provides educators, parents, and after-school professionals with access to high-quality practices in reading and language arts instruction by offering the very best in free materials.
ReadWriteThink
c/o NCTE
1111 W. Kenyon Rd.
Urbana, IL 61801
Internet address: http://www.readwritethink.org

2. ONLINE CHILDREN'S BOOKS LISTS

California Recommended Literature
Collection of outstanding literature for children and adolescents in grades kindergarten through grade 12.
http://www.cde.ca.gov/ci/rl/ll/index.asp

New York Public Library
"On-Lion" for Kids
Comprehensive web site for librarians, parents, and educators
Internet address: http://kids.nypl.org/index.cfm

Reading Is Fundamental
Reading Is Fundamental, Inc. prepares and motivates children to read by delivering free books and literacy resources to those children and families who need them most, with a focus on birth through age 11. Includes bilingual resources.
Internet address: http://www.rif.org/

Reading Rockets
Children's Books & Authors
Multiple categories of children's books and authors are suggested.
Internet address: https://www.readingrockets.org/books

San Diego Public Library
Kids and Teens
Internet address: https://www.sandiego.gov/public-library/kidsandteens

Texas State Library and Archives Commission
Resources for Selecting Bilingual and Spanish Children's Books
Internet address: http://www.tsl.state.tx.us/ld/projects/ninos/profres.html
Additional Reading Activities
Internet address: http://www.tsl.state.tx.us/ld/projects/trc/rdactivities.html

3. ONLINE DICTIONARIES FOR PARENTS, TEACHERS, AND STUDENTS

Kids.Wordsmyth
Internet address: https://kids.wordsmyth.net/we/

Southwest Educational Development Laboratory
Glossary of Reading-related Terms:
Internet address: http://www.sedl.org/reading/framework/glossary.html

Longman Dictionary of Contemporary English Online
Internet address: http://www.ldoceonline.com

Merriam-Webster Dictionary
Online dictionary and thesaurus for children and adults.
Internet address: http://www.m-w.com
Online dictionary for children.
Internet address: http://www.wordcentral.com

Appendix C

Introduction to National K-5 Common Core State Standards

Common Core State Standards for English Language Arts & Literacy in History/Social Studies, Science, and Technical Subjects

Introduction to Common Core State Standards

http://www.corestandards.org/

About the Standards

SOURCE: http://www.corestandards.org/about-the-standards. © Copyright 2010. National Governors Association Center for Best Practices and Council of Chief State School Officers. All rights reserved.

The Common Core State Standards Initiative is a state-led effort coordinated by the National Governors Association Center for Best Practices (NGA Center) and the Council of Chief State School Officers (CCSSO). The standards were developed in collaboration with teachers, school administrators, and experts to provide a clear and consistent framework to prepare our children for college and the workforce.

The NGA Center and CCSSO received initial feedback on the draft standards from national organizations representing, but not limited to, teachers, postsecondary educators (including community colleges), civil rights groups, English language learners, and students with disabilities. Following the initial round of feedback, the draft standards were opened for public comment, receiving nearly 10,000 responses.

The standards are informed by the highest, most effective models from states across the country and countries around the world, and provide teachers and parents with a common understanding of what students are expected to learn. Consistent standards will provide appropriate benchmarks for all students, regardless of where they live.

These standards define the knowledge and skills students should have within their K-12 education careers so that they will graduate high school able to succeed in entry-level, credit-bearing academic college courses and in workforce training programs. The standards:

- Are aligned with college and work expectations;

- Are clear, understandable, and consistent;

- Include rigorous content and application of knowledge through high-order skills;

- Build upon strengths and lessons of current state standards;

- Are informed by other top-performing countries, so that all students are prepared to succeed in our global economy and society; and

- Are evidence-based.

Mission Statement:

SOURCE: http://www.corestandards.org/. © Copyright 2010. National Governors Association Center for Best Practices and Council of Chief State School Officers. All rights reserved.

The Common Core State Standards provide a consistent, clear understanding of what students are expected to learn, so teachers and parents know what they need to do to help them. The standards are designed to be robust and relevant to the real world, reflecting the knowledge and skills that our young people need for success in college and careers. With American students fully prepared for the future, our communities will be best positioned to compete successfully in the global economy.

Building on the excellent foundation of standards states have laid, the Common Core State Standards are the first step in providing our young people with a high-quality education. It should be clear to every student, parent, and teacher what the standards of success are in every school.

What Is Not Covered by the Standards

SOURCE: http://www.corestandards.org/assets/CCSSI_ELA%20Standards.pdf (page 6). © Copyright 2010. National Governors Association Center for Best Practices and Council of Chief State School Officers. All rights reserved.

1. The Standards define what all students are expected to know and be able to do, not how teachers should teach.

2. While the Standards focus on what is most essential, they do not describe all that can or should be taught.

3. The Standards do not define the nature of advanced work for students who meet the Standards prior to the end of high school.

4. The Standards set grade-specific standards but do not define the intervention methods or materials necessary to support students who are well below or well above grade-level expectations.

5. It is also beyond the scope of the Standards to define the full range of supports appropriate for English language learners and for students with special needs.

6. While the ELA and content area literacy components described herein are critical to college and career readiness, they do not define the whole of such readiness.

The California Department of Education provides translations of the Common Core State Standards in Spanish, Chinese, and Vietnamese: https://inet2.cde.ca.gov/cmd/translatedparentaldoc.aspx?docid=6950-6957

Common Core Standards for English Language Arts & Literacy in History/Social Studies, Science, and Technical Subjects

SOURCE: https://ccsso.org/resource-library/ada-compliant-ela-standards. © Copyright 2010. National Governors Association Center for Best Practices and Council of Chief State School Officers. All rights reserved.

The Common Core State Standards for English Language Arts & Literacy in History/Social Studies, Science, and Technical Subjects ("the Standards") are the culmination of an extended, broad-based effort to fulfill the charge issued by the states to create the next generation of K–12 standards in order to help ensure that all students are college- and career-ready in literacy no later than the end of high school.

The Standards set requirements not only for English language arts (ELA) but also for literacy in history/social studies, science, and technical subjects. Just as students must learn to read, write, speak, listen, and use language effectively in a variety of content areas, so too must the Standards specify the literacy skills and understandings required for college and career readiness in multiple disciplines.

Appendix D

Strategies and Goals

Parents and educators are encouraged to plan each strategy in Part 3 to intentionally address kindergarten through grade five expectations such as the *Common Core State Standards for English Language Arts and Literacy in History/Social Studies, Science, and Technical Subjects K-5*. Appendix E suggests examples of CCSS/ELA K-5 standards for each strategy in Part 3: *Strategies with a Purpose.*

Refer to the complete documents for grade-specific descriptions and further information:

Common Core State Standards (CCSS) document for grade-specific description and
further information: http://www.corestandards.org/the-standards/english-
language-arts-standards

The California Department of Education offers the CCSS documents in Spanish,
Chinese, and Vietnamese. https://inet2.cde.ca.gov/cmd/translatedparentaldoc.
aspx?docid=6950-6957

Common Core State Standards

Reading Standards: Foundational Skills (K–5)

Common Core State Standards for English Language Arts & Literacy in History/Social Studies, Science, and Technical Subjects
SOURCE: http://www.corestandards.org/assets/CCSSI_ELA%20Standards.pdf (pages 15-17).
© Copyright 2010. National Governors Association Center for Best Practices and Council of Chief State School Officers. All rights reserved.*

The Reading Standards Foundational Skills K-5 (RF) are directed toward fostering students' understanding and working knowledge of concepts of print, the alphabetic principle, and other basic conventions of the English writing system. These foundational skills are not an end in and of themselves; rather, they are necessary and important components of an effective, comprehensive reading program designed to develop proficient readers with the capacity to comprehend texts across a range of types and disciplines. Instruction should be differentiated: good readers will need much less practice with these concepts than struggling readers will. The point is to teach students what they need to learn and not what they already know—to discern when particular children or activities warrant more or less attention (*Common Core State Standards*, p. 15)

Literacy-Reading: Foundational Skills

ABC Book – page 30

Kindergarten-Grade 2:
CCSS English Language Arts & Literacy- Reading Standards: Foundational Skills
- *Print Concepts 1. Demonstrate understanding of the organization and basic features of print. 1d. Recognize and name all upper- and lowercase letters of the alphabet.*
- *Phonics and Word recognition 3. Know and apply grade-level phonics and word analysis skills in decoding words 3a. Demonstrate basic knowledge of one-to-one letter-sound correspondences by producing the primary or many of the most frequent sounds for each consonant.*
Grade 1: *Phonics and Word Recognition 3. Know and apply grade-level phonics and word analysis skills in decoding words. b. Decode regularly spelled one-syllable words.*
Grade 2: *Phonics and Word*

Recognitio 3. Know and apply grade-level phonics and word analysis skills in decoding words. a. Distinguish long and short vowels when reading regularly spelled one-syllable words.

Alpha – page 33

Kindergarten:
CCSS English Language Arts & Literacy- Reading Standards: Foundational Skills
Print Concepts 1. Demonstrate understanding of the organization and basic features of print. 1d. Recognize and name all upper- and lowercase letters of the alphabet.

Kindergarten-Grade 1:
CCSS English Language Arts & Literacy: Language
- Kindergarten: *Conventions of Standard English 1. Demonstrate command of the conventions of standard English grammar and usage when writing or speaking. 1a. Print many upper- and lowercase letters.*
- Grade 1: *Conventions of Standard English 1. Print all upper- and lowercase letters.*

Breaking Up Is Hard to Do – page 35

Kindergarten-Grade 1:
CCSS English Language Arts & Literacy- Reading Standards: Foundational Skills
- *Phonological Awareness 2c: Demonstrate understanding of spoken words, syllables, and sounds (phonemes)-Blend and segment onsets and rimes of single-syllable spoken words.*
- *Grade 1: Phonological Awareness 2b. Orally produce single-syllable words by blending sounds (phonemes), including consonant blends.*

Clapping Machines – page 36

Kindergarten-Grade 1:
CCSS English Language Arts & Literacy- Reading Standards: Foundational Skills
- *Kindergarten: Phonological Awareness 2b: Demonstrate understanding of spoken words, syllables, and sounds (phonemes)- Count, pronounce, blend, and segment syllables in spoken words.*
- *Grade 1: Phonological Awareness 2. Demonstrate*

*Common Core State Standards correlated to author's activity sheets.

understanding of spoken words, syllables, and sounds (phonemes)

Do You Hear an Echo? – page 37

Kindergarten-Grade 5
CCSS English Language Arts & Literacy- Reading Standards: Foundational Skills

- Kindergarten: *Fluency 4. Read emergent-reader texts with purpose and understanding.*
- Grades 1-5: *Fluency 4. Read with sufficient accuracy and fluency to support comprehension.*

Drivin' to the Beat – page 38

Kindergarten:
CCSS English Language Arts & Literacy- Reading Standards: Foundational Skills

- *Phonological Awareness 2a: Recognize and produce rhyming words.*

Finger Walk – page 39

Kindergarten-Grade 1:
CCSS English Language Arts & Literacy- Reading Standards: Foundational Skills

- Kindergarten *Print Concepts 1. Demonstrate understanding of the organization and basic features of print. 1c: Understand that words are separated by spaces in print.*
Grade 1: *Print Concepts 1. Demonstrate understanding of the organization and basic features of print.*
a. *Recognize the distinguishing features of a sentence (e.g., first word, capitalization, ending punctuation).*

Fun on Board – page 40

Kindergarten:
CCSS English Language Arts & Literacy- Reading Standards: Foundational Skills

- *Print Concepts 1d. Recognize and name all upper- and lowercase letters of the alphabet.*

Green Means Go – page 41

Kindergarten:
CCSS English Language Arts & Literacy- Reading Standards: Foundational Skills

- *Print Concepts 1. Demonstrate understanding of the organization and basic features of print. 1a. Follow words from left to right, top to bottom, and page by page.*

In the Bag – page 42

Kindergarten:
CCSS English Language Arts & Literacy- Reading Standards: Foundational Skills

- *Print Concepts 1. Demonstrate understanding of the organization and basic features of print. 1d. Recognize and name all upper- and lowercase letters of the alphabet.*

Kindergarten-Grade 2:
CCSS English Language Arts & Literacy- Reading Standards: Foundational Skills

- *Phonics and Word recognition 3. Know and apply grade-level phonics and word analysis skills in decoding words.*
- *Kindergarten: 3a: Demonstrate basic knowledge of one-to-one letter-sound correspondences by producing the primary sound for each consonant.*

Is It Too Hard? – page 43

Kindergarten-Grade 5:
CCSS English Language Arts & Literacy- Reading Standards: Foundational Skills

- Kindergarten *Fluency 4. Read emergent-reader texts with purpose and understanding.*
- Grades 1-5 *Fluency 4. Read with sufficient accuracy and fluency to support comprehension.*

Joking Around – page 44

Kindergarten-Grade 5:
CCSS English Language Arts & Literacy- Reading Standards: Foundational Skills

- Kindergarten: *Fluency 4. Read emergent-reader texts with purpose and understanding.*
- Grades 1-5: *Fluency 4. Read with sufficient accuracy and fluency to support comprehension. 4c. Use context to confirm or self-correct word recognition and understanding, rereading as necessary*

Land on It! – page 45

Grade 1:
CCSS English Language Arts & Literacy- Reading Standards: Foundational Skills

- Grade One *Phonics and Word recognition 3a. Know the spelling-sound correspondences for common consonant digraphs.*

Leave It Out – page 47

Kindergarten-Grade 5:
CCSS English Language Arts & Literacy: Language

- Kindergarten-Grade 5: *Vocabulary acquisition and Use 4. Determine or clarify the meaning of unknown and multiple-meaning words and phrases based on grade level reading and content.*
- Grades 1-3: *4a. Use sentence-level context as a clue to the meaning of a word or phrase.*
- Grades 4-5: *4a. Use context (e.g., definitions, examples, or restatements in text; cause/effect relationships and comparisons in text) as a clue to the meaning of a word or phrase.*

Letter Art – page 48

Kindergarten:
CCSS English Language Arts & Literacy- Reading Standards: Foundational Skills

- *Phonics and Word recognition 3a. Demonstrate basic knowledge of one-to-one letter-sound correspondences by producing the primary or many of the most frequent sound for each consonant.*

Make a Game of It – page 49

Kindergarten-Grade 2:
CCSS English Language Arts & Literacy: Speaking and Listening

- Kindergarten: *Comprehension and Collaboration 2. Confirm understanding of a text read aloud or information presented orally or through other media by asking and answering questions about key details and requesting clarification if something is not understood.*

- Grades 1-2: *Comprehension and Collaboration 2. Ask and answer questions about key details in a text read aloud or information presented orally or through other media.*

Make a Match – page 50

Kindergarten-Grade 1:
CCSS English Language Arts & Literacy- Reading Standards: Foundational Skills
- *Print Concepts 1. Demonstrate understanding of the organization and basic features of print. 1d. Recognize and name all upper- and lowercase letters of the alphabet.*
Grade 1: *Print Concepts 1. Demonstrate understanding of the organization and basic features of print. a. Recognize the distinguishing features of a sentence (e.g., first word, capitalization, ending punctuation).*

More Fun Than One – page 51

Grades 3–5:
CCSS English Language Arts & Literacy- Reading Standards: Foundational Skills
- Grades 3-5: *Fluency 4. Read with sufficient accuracy and fluency to support comprehension. 4b. Read on-level prose and poetry orally with accuracy, appropriate rate, and expression on successive readings.*

Mystery Word – page 52

Kindergarten-Grade 5
CCSS English Language Arts & Literacy- Reading Standards: Foundational Skills
- *Phonics and Word recognition 3. Know and apply grade-level phonics and word analysis skills in decoding words*
- Grade 1: *3b. Decode regularly spelled one-syllable words. 3e. Decode two-syllable words following basic patterns by breaking words into syllables.*
- Grade 2: *3c. Decode regularly spelled two-syllable words with long vowels. 3d. Decode words with common prefixes and suffixes.*

- Grade 3: *3c. Decode multisyllable words.*
- Grades 4 & 5: *3a. Use combined knowledge of all letter-sound correspondences, syllabication patterns, and morphemes (e.g., roots and affixes) to read accurately unfamiliar multisyllable words in context and out of context.*

Record It – page 53

Kindergarten–Grade 5:
CCSS English Language Arts & Literacy- Reading Standards: Foundational Skills
- Kindergarten: *Fluency 4. Read emergent-reader texts with purpose and understanding.*
- Grades 1-5: *Fluency 4. Read with sufficient accuracy and fluency to support comprehension. 4a. Read on-level text with purpose and understanding.*

Seeing and Saying Key Words – page 54

Kindergarten-Grade 1:
CCSS English Language Arts & Literacy- Reading Standards: Foundational Skills
Kindergarten: CCSS Reading Standards: Foundational Skills Print Concepts: 1b: Recognize that spoken words are represented in written language by specific sequence of letters
Grade 1 Phonological Awareness: 2a. Distinguish long from short vowel sounds in spoken single-syllable words.

Kindergarten-Grade 5:
CCSS English Language Arts & Literacy- Reading Standards: Foundational Skills
- *Phonics and Word recognition 3. Know and apply grade-level phonics and word analysis skills in decoding words.*

Seeing How We Read and Write Sentences – page 56

Kindergarten:
CCSS English Language Arts & Literacy- Reading Standards: Foundational Skills
- *Print Concepts 1. Demonstrate understanding of the organization and basic features*

of print. 1a. Follow words from left to right, top to bottom, and page by page.
CCSS Reading Standards: Foundational Skills
- Grade 1: *Print Concepts: 1a. Recognize the distinguishing features of a sentence such as first word, capitalization, ending punctuation.*

Shop 'Til You Drop – page 57

Kindergarten–Grade 5:
CCSS English Language Arts & Literacy- Reading Standards: Foundational Skills
- *Phonics and Word recognition 3. Know and apply grade-level phonics and word analysis skills in decoding words.*

Shopping for Words – page 58

Kindergarten–Grade 1:
CCSS English Language Arts & Literacy: Language
- *Vocabulary acquisition and Use 5. With guidance and support from adults, explore word relationships and nuances in word meanings.*

Kindergarten–Grade 5:
CCSS English Language Arts & Literacy- Reading Standards: Foundational Skills
- *Phonics and Word recognition 3. Know and apply grade-level phonics and word analysis skills in decoding words.*
- **Grades 4-5:** 3a. Use combined knowledge of letter-sounds, syllabic patters, and more to read accurately unfamiliar multisyllable words in context and out of context

• Shout It and Write It—I'm So Proud! – page 59

Kindergarten-Grade 5:
CCSS English Language Arts & Literacy- Reading Standards: Foundational Skills
- *Kindergarten-Grade 1: Phonological Awareness: Demonstrate understanding of spoken words, syllables, and sounds (phonemes).*
- *Kindergarten-Grade 5: Phonics and Word Recognition: Know and apply grade level phonics and word recognition skills in decoding words.*

Silly Sounds – page 60

Kindergarten–Grade 1:
CCSS English Language Arts & Literacy- Reading Standards: Foundational Skills

- *Phonological Awareness K-1: 2 Demonstrate understanding of spoken words, syllables, and sounds (phonemes)- K: 2b Count, pronounce, blend, and segment syllables in spoken words.*
- *K: 2e: Add or substitute individual sounds (phonemes) in simple, one-syllable words to make new words*
- Grade 1: *Phonological Awareness 2b: Orally produce single-syllable words by blending sounds (phonemes), including consonant blends.*

Tap Dancer – page 61

Kindergarten:
CCSS English Language Arts & Literacy- Reading Standards: Foundational Skills (K–5)

- *Phonological Awareness 2b: Demonstrate understanding of spoken words, syllables, and sounds (phonemes)- Count, pronounce, blend, and segment syllables in spoken words.*

Trace-Over Art – page 62

Kindergarten
CCSS English Language Arts & Literacy- Reading Standards: Foundational Skills

- *Print Concepts 1. Demonstrate understanding of the organization and basic features of print. 1d. Recognize and name all upper- and lowercase letters of the alphabet.*

Kindergarten-Grade 1
CCSS English Language Arts & Literacy: Language

- Kindergarten: *Conventions of Standard English 1. Demonstrate command of the conventions of standard English grammar and usage when writing or speaking. 1a. Print many upper- and lowercase letters.*
- Grade 1: *Conventions of Standard English 1. Print all upper- and lowercase letters.*

What a Character! – page 63

Kindergarten-Grade 5:
CCSS English Language Arts & Literacy- Reading Standards: Foundational Skills

- Kindergarten: *Fluency 4. Read emergent-reader texts with purpose and understanding.*
- Grades 1-5: *Fluency 4. Read with sufficient accuracy and fluency to support comprehension.*

Wonderful Words – page 64

Kindergarten-Grade 1:
CCSS English Language Arts & Literacy- Reading Standards: Foundational Skills

- Kindergarten-Grade 1: *1. Phonological Awareness - Demonstrate understanding of spoken words, syllables, and sounds (phonemes)*

Word Speed-Up – page 65

Kindergarten-Grade 5:
CCSS English Language Arts & Literacy- Reading Standards: Foundational Skills

- *Phonics and Word recognition K–5 3. Know and apply grade-level phonics and word analysis skills in decoding words.*
- Kindergarten (3c): Read common high-frequency words by sight such as *the, of, to, you, she my, is, are, do , does).*
- Grades 1(3g), Grade 2 (3f): *Recognize and read grade-appropriate irregular spelling words.*
- Grade 3 (3d): *Read grade-appropriate irregularly spelled words.*

Common Core State Standards

Speaking & Listening Standards K-5 (SL)

Common Core State Standards for English Language Arts & Literacy in History/Social Studies, Science, and Technical Subjects
SOURCE: http://www.corestandards.org/assets/CCSSI_ELA%20Standards.pdf (pages 22-24).
© Copyright 2010. National Governors Association Center for Best Practices and Council of Chief State School Officers. All rights reserved.*

Speaking and Listening standards for K–5 offer a focus for instruction each year to help ensure that students gain adequate mastery of a range of skills and applications.

Students advancing through the grades are expected to meet each year's grade-specific standards and retain or further develop skills and understandings mastered in preceding grades. (*Common Core State Standards*, p. 23)

Speaking & Listening

Ask More and Tell Less – page 70

Kindergarten-Grade 3:
CCSS English Language Arts & Literacy: Speaking and Listening
- Kindergarten: *Comprehension and Collaboration 3. Ask and answer questions in order to seek help, get information, or clarify something that is not understood.*
- Grade 1: *Comprehension and Collaboration 3. Ask and answer questions about what a speaker says in order to gather additional information or clarify something that is not understood.*
- Grade 2: *Comprehension and Collaboration 3. Ask and answer questions about what a speaker says in order to clarify comprehension, gather additional information, or deepen understanding of a topic or issue.*
- Grade 3: *Comprehension and Collaboration 3. Ask and answer questions about information from a speaker, offering appropriate elaboration and detail.*

Career Field Trip – page 71

Kindergarten-Grade 5:
CCSS English Language Arts & Literacy: Speaking and Listening
- Kindergarten: *Comprehension and Collaboration 2. Confirm understanding of a text read aloud or information presented orally or through other media by asking and answering questions about key details and requesting clarification if something is not understood. 3. Ask and answer questions in order to seek help, get information, or clarify something that is not understood.*
- Grade 1 & 2: *Comprehension and Collaboration 2. Ask and answer questions about key details in a text read aloud or information presented orally or through other media. 3. Ask and answer questions about what a speaker says in order to gather additional information.*
- Grade 3: *Comprehension and Collaboration 2. Determine the main ideas and supporting details of a text read aloud or information presented in diverse media and formats, including visually, quantitatively, and orally... 3. Ask and answer questions about information from a speaker, offering appropriate elaboration and detail.*
- Grade 4: *Comprehension and Collaboration 2. Paraphrase portions of a text read aloud or information presented in diverse media and formats, including visually, quantitatively, and orally.*
- Grade 5: *Comprehension and Collaboration 2. Summarize a written text read aloud or information presented in diverse media and formats, including visually, quantitatively, and orally.*

Check, Please! – page 72

Kindergarten-Grade 5:
CCSS English Language Arts & Literacy: Speaking and Listening
- Kindergarten: *Presentation of Knowledge and Ideas 6. Speak audibly and express thoughts, feelings, and ideas clearly.*
- Grade 1: *Presentation of Knowledge and Ideas 6. Produce complete sentences when appropriate to task and situation.*
- Grade 2: *Presentation of Knowledge and Ideas 6. Produce complete sentences when appropriate to task and situation in order to provide requested detail or clarification.*
- Grade 3: *Presentation of Knowledge and Ideas 6. Speak in complete sentences when appropriate to task and situation in order to provide requested detail or clarification.*
- Grade 4: *Presentation of Knowledge and Ideas 6. Differentiate between contexts that call for formal English (e.g., presenting ideas) and situations where informal discourse is appropriate (e.g., small-group discussion); use formal English when appropriate to task and situation.*

- Grade 5: *Presentation of Knowledge and Ideas 6. Adapt speech to a variety of contexts and tasks, using formal English when appropriate to task and situation.*

Child Chat – page 73

Kindergarten-Grade 5:
CCSS English Language Arts & Literacy: Speaking and Listening
- Grades K-2 *Comprehension and Collaboration 1. Participate in collaborative conversations with diverse partners about grade-appropriate topics and texts with peers and adults in small and larger groups.*
- Grades 3-5: *Comprehension and Collaboration 1. Engage effectively in a range of collaborative discussions (one-on-one, in groups, and teacher-led) with diverse partners discussing grade-appropriate topics and texts, building on others' ideas and expressing their own clearly.*

Draw a Word – page 74

Kindergarten-Grade 5:
CCSS English Language Arts & Literacy: Language
- K-Grade 1: *Vocabulary acquisition and Use 5. With guidance and support from adults, explore word relationships and nuances in word meanings.*
- Grades 2-5: *Vocabulary acquisition and Use 5. Demonstrate understanding of figurative language, word relationships, and nuances in word meanings.*

Kindergarten-Grade 2:
CCSS English Language Arts & Literacy: Speaking and Listening
- Grade K: *Presentation of Knowledge and Ideas 5. Add drawings or other visual displays to descriptions as desired to provide additional detail.*
- Grade 1: *Presentation of Knowledge and Ideas 5. Add drawings or other visual displays to descriptions when appropriate to clarify ideas, thoughts, and feelings.*
- Grade 2: *Presentation of Knowledge and Ideas 5. Create*

audio recordings of stories or poems; add drawings or other visual displays to stories or recounts of experiences when appropriate to clarify ideas, thoughts, and feelings.

Going to the Doctor – page 76

Kindergarten-Grade 5:
CCSS English Language Arts & Literacy: Speaking and Listening
- Kindergarten: *Presentation of Knowledge and Ideas 4. Describe familiar people, places, things, and events and, with prompting and support, provide additional detail.*
- Grade 1: *Presentation of Knowledge and Ideas 4. Describe people, places, things, and events with relevant details, expressing ideas and feelings clearly.*
- Grade 2: *Presentation of Knowledge and Ideas 4. Tell a story or recount an experience with appropriate facts and relevant, descriptive details, speaking audibly in coherent sentences.*
- Grades 3 & 4: *Presentation of Knowledge and Ideas 4. Report on a topic or text, tell a story, or recount an experience with appropriate facts and relevant, descriptive details, speaking clearly at an understandable pace.*
- Grade 5: Grades 3 & 4. *Presentation of Knowledge and Ideas 4. Report on a topic or text or present an opinion, sequencing ideas logically and using appropriate facts and relevant, descriptive details to support main ideas or themes; speak clearly at an understandable pace.*

Hear It First – page 77

Kindergarten-Grade 5:
CCSS English Language Arts & Literacy: Speaking and Listening
- Kindergarten: *Comprehension and Collaboration 2. Confirm understanding of a text read aloud or information presented orally or through other media by asking and answering questions about key details and requesting*

clarification if something is not understood. 3. Ask and answer questions in order to seek help, get information, or clarify something that is not understood.
- Grade 1 & 2: *Comprehension and Collaboration 2. Ask and answer questions about key details in a text read aloud or information presented orally or through other media. 3. Ask and answer questions about what a speaker says in order to gather additional information.*
- Grade 3: *Comprehension and Collaboration 2. Determine the main ideas and supporting details of a text read aloud or information presented in diverse media and formats, including visually, quantitatively, and orally.*
- Grade 4: *Comprehension and Collaboration 2. Paraphrase portions of a text read aloud or information presented in diverse media and formats, including visually, quantitatively, and orally.*
- Grade 5: *Comprehension and Collaboration 2. Summarize a written text read aloud or information presented in diverse media and formats, including visually, quantitatively, and orally.*

Hide and Guess – page 79

Kindergarten-Grade 3:
CCSS English Language Arts & Literacy: Speaking and Listening
- Kindergarten: *Comprehension and Collaboration 3. Ask and answer questions in order to seek help, get information, or clarify something that is not understood.*
- Grade 1: *Comprehension and Collaboration 3. Ask and answer questions about what a speaker says in order to gather additional information or clarify something that is not understood.*
- Grade 2: *Comprehension and Collaboration 3. Ask and answer questions about what a speaker says in order to clarify comprehension, gather additional information, or deepen understanding of a topic or issue.*
- Grade 3: *Comprehension and*

Collaboration 3. Ask and answer questions about information from a speaker, offering appropriate elaboration and detail.

Lights, Camera, Action! – page 80

Grades 2-5:
CCSS English Language Arts & Literacy: Speaking and Listening

- Grade 2: *Presentation of Knowledge and Ideas 5. Create audio recordings of stories or poems; add drawings or other visual displays to stories or recounts of experiences when appropriate to clarify ideas, thoughts, and feelings.*
- Grade 3: *Presentation of Knowledge and Ideas 5. Create engaging audio recordings of stories or poems that demonstrate fluid reading at an understandable pace; add visual displays when appropriate to emphasize or enhance certain facts or details.*
- Grade 4: *Presentation of Knowledge and Ideas 5. Add audio recordings and visual displays to presentations when appropriate to enhance the development of main ideas or themes.*
- Grade 5: *Presentation of Knowledge and Ideas 5. Include multimedia components (e.g., graphics, sound) and visual displays in presentations when appropriate to enhance the development of main ideas or themes.*

News Reporter – page 81

Kindergarten-Grade 5:
CCSS English Language Arts & Literacy: Speaking and Listening

- Kindergarten: *Presentation of Knowledge and Ideas 6. Speak audibly and express thoughts, feelings, and ideas clearly.*
- Grade 1: *Presentation of Knowledge and Ideas 6. Produce complete sentences when appropriate to task and situation.*
- Grade 2: *Presentation of Knowledge and Ideas 6. Produce complete sentences when appropriate to task and situation*

in order to provide requested detail or clarification.
- Grade 3: *Presentation of Knowledge and Ideas 6. Speak in complete sentences when appropriate to task and situation in order to provide requested detail or clarification.*
- Grade 4: *Presentation of Knowledge and Ideas 6. Differentiate between contexts that call for formal English (e.g., presenting ideas) and situations where informal discourse is appropriate (e.g., small-group discussion); use formal English when appropriate to task and situation.*
- Grade 5: *Presentation of Knowledge and Ideas 6. Adapt speech to a variety of contexts and tasks, using formal English when appropriate to task and situation.*

Kindergarten-Grade 5:
CCSS English Language Arts & Literacy: Language

- *Conventions of Standard English 1. Demonstrate command of the conventions of standard English grammar and usage when writing or speaking.*

Parent/Student/Teacher Meeting – page 82

Grades 1-5:
CCSS English Language Arts & Literacy: Speaking and Listening - Comprehension and Collaboration

- Grade 1: *Ask questions to clear up confusion about the topic and texts under consideration.*
- Grade 2: *Ask for clarification and further information as needed about the topics and texts under discussion.*
- Grade 3: *Ask questions to check understanding of information presented, stay on topic, and link the comments to the remarks of others.*
- Grades 4-5: *Pose and respond to specific questions to clarify or follow-up on information, and make comments that contribute to the discussion and link to the remarks of others.*

Play-by-Play – page 84

Kindergarten-Grade 5:
CCSS English Language Arts & Literacy: Speaking and Listening

- Kindergarten: *Presentation of Knowledge and Ideas 4. Describe familiar people, places, things, and events and, with prompting and support, provide additional detail.*
- Grade 1: *Presentation of Knowledge and Ideas 4. Describe people, places, things, and events with relevant details, expressing ideas and feelings clearly.*
- Grade 2: *Presentation of Knowledge and Ideas 4. Tell a story or recount an experience with appropriate facts and relevant, descriptive details, speaking audibly in coherent sentences.*
- Grades 3 & 4: *Presentation of Knowledge and Ideas 4. Report on a topic or text, tell a story, or recount an experience with appropriate facts and relevant, descriptive details, speaking clearly at an understandable pace.*
- Grade 5: *Grades 3 & 4. Presentation of Knowledge and Ideas 4. Report on a topic or text or present an opinion, sequencing ideas logically and using appropriate facts and relevant, descriptive details to support main ideas or themes; speak clearly at an understandable pace.*

Question and Answer Time – page 85

Kindergarten-Grade 3:
CCSS English Language Arts & Literacy: Speaking and Listening

- Kindergarten: *Comprehension and Collaboration 3. Ask and answer questions in order to seek help, get information, or clarify something that is not understood.*
- Grade 1: *Comprehension and Collaboration 3. Ask and answer questions about what a speaker says in order to gather additional information or clarify something that is not understood.*
- Grade 2: *Comprehension and Collaboration 3. Ask and answer*

questions about what a speaker says in order to clarify comprehension, gather additional information, or deepen understanding of a topic or issue.
- Grade 3: *Comprehension and Collaboration 3. Ask and answer questions about information from a speaker, offering appropriate elaboration and detail.*

Say It Like You Mean It – page 86

Kindergarten-Grade 5:
CCSS English Language Arts & Literacy: Speaking and Listening
- Grade K: *Presentation of Knowledge and Ideas 5. Add drawings or other visual displays to descriptions as desired to provide additional detail.*
- Grade 1: *Presentation of Knowledge and Ideas 5. Add drawings or other visual displays to descriptions when appropriate to clarify ideas, thoughts, and feelings.*
- Grade 2: *Presentation of Knowledge and Ideas 5. Create audio recordings of stories or poems; add drawings or other visual displays to stories or recounts of experiences when appropriate to clarify ideas, thoughts, and feelings.*
- Grade 3: *Presentation of Knowledge and Ideas 5. Create engaging audio recordings of stories or poems that demonstrate fluid reading at an understandable pace; add visual displays when appropriate to emphasize or enhance certain facts or details.*
- Grade 4: *Presentation of Knowledge and Ideas 5. Add audio recordings and visual displays to presentations when*

appropriate to enhance the development of main ideas or themes.
- Grade 5: *Presentation of Knowledge and Ideas 5. Include multimedia components (e.g., graphics, sound) and visual displays in presentations when appropriate to enhance the development of main ideas or themes.*

Take Charge – page 87

Kindergarten-Grade 5:
CCSS English Language Arts & Literacy: Speaking and Listening
- Grades K-2 *Comprehension and Collaboration 1. Participate in collaborative conversations with diverse partners about grade-appropriate topics and texts with peers and adults in small and larger groups.*
- Grades 3-5: *Comprehension and Collaboration 1. Engage effectively in a range of collaborative discussions (one-on-one, in groups, and teacher-led) with diverse partners discussing grade-appropriate topics and texts, building on others' ideas and expressing their own clearly.*

Tell Me More – page 89

Kindergarten-Grade 5:
CCSS English Language Arts & Literacy: Speaking and Listening
- Grades K-2 *Comprehension and Collaboration 1. Participate in collaborative conversations with diverse partners about grade-appropriate topics and texts with peers and adults in small and larger groups.*
- Grades 3-5: *Comprehension and Collaboration 1. Engage effectively in a range of collaborative discussions (one-on-*

one, in groups, and teacher-led) with diverse partners discussing grade-appropriate topics and texts, building on others' ideas and expressing their own clearly.

Kindergarten-Grade 5:
CCSS English Language Arts & Literacy: Speaking and Listening
- Kindergarten: *Comprehension and Collaboration 2. Confirm understanding of a text read aloud or information presented orally or through other media by asking and answering questions about key details and requesting clarification if something is not understood.*
- Grades 1-2: *Comprehension and Collaboration 2. Ask and answer questions about key details in a text read aloud or information presented orally or through other media.*
- Grade 3: *Comprehension and Collaboration 2. Determine the main ideas and supporting details of a text read aloud or information presented in diverse media and formats, including visually, quantitatively, and orally… 3. Ask and answer questions about information from a speaker, offering appropriate elaboration and detail.*
- Grade 4: *Comprehension and Collaboration 2. Paraphrase portions of a text read aloud or information presented in diverse media and formats, including visually, quantitatively, and orally.*
- Grade 5: *Comprehension and Collaboration 2. Summarize a written text read aloud or information presented in diverse media and formats, including visually, quantitatively, and orally.*

Common Core State Standards

Language Standards (L)

Common Core State Standards for English Language Arts & Literacy in History/Social Studies, Science, and Technical Subjects
SOURCE: http://www.corestandards.org/assets/CCSSI_ELA%20Standards.pdf (pages 25-30).
© Copyright 2010. National Governors Association Center for Best Practices and Council of Chief State School Officers. All rights reserved.*

Language standards for grades K–5 offer a focus for instruction each year to help ensure that students gain adequate mastery of a range of skills and applications. Students advancing through the grades are expected to meet each year's grade-specific standards and retain or further develop skills and understandings mastered in preceding grades. (*Common Core State Standards,* p. 26)

Language

At Close Range – page 93

Kindergarten-Grade 1:
CCSS English Language Arts & Literacy: Language
- Kindergarten: *Conventions of Standard English 1. Demonstrate command of the conventions of standard English grammar and usage when writing or speaking. 1a. Print many upper- and lowercase letters.*
- Grade 1: *Conventions of Standard English 1. Print all upper- and lowercase letters.*

Call It as You See It – page 94

Kindergarten-Grade 1
CCSS English Language Arts & Literacy: Language
- Kindergarten: *Conventions of Standard English 1. Demonstrate command of the conventions of standard English grammar and usage when writing or speaking. 1a. Print many upper- and lowercase letters.*
- Grade 1: *Conventions of Standard English 1. Print all upper- and lowercase letters.*

Charted Letters – page 95

Kindergarten-Grade 1:
CCSS English Language Arts & Literacy: Language
- Kindergarten: *Conventions of Standard English 1. Demonstrate command of the conventions of standard English grammar and usage when writing or speaking. 1a. Print many upper- and lowercase letters.*
- Grade 1: *Conventions of Standard English 1. Print all upper- and lowercase letters.*

Cleaning Day Fun – page 97

Kindergarten-Grade 1:
CCSS English Language Arts & Literacy: Language
- *Vocabulary acquisition and Use 5. With guidance and support from adults, explore word relationships and nuances in word meanings. 5a. Sort common objects into categories (e.g., shapes, foods … colors, clothing …) to gain a sense of the concepts the categories represent.*

Computer Fun with New Words – page 98

Kindergarten-Grade 1:
CCSS English Language Arts & Literacy: Language
- *Vocabulary acquisition and Use 5. With guidance and support from adults, explore word relationships and nuances in word meanings.*

Kindergarten-Grade 2:
CCSS English Language Arts & Literacy: Speaking and Listening
- *Grade K: Presentation of Knowledge and Ideas 5. Add drawings or other visual displays to descriptions as desired to provide additional detail.*
- Grade 1: *Presentation of Knowledge and Ideas 5. Add drawings or other visual displays to descriptions when appropriate to clarify ideas, thoughts, and feelings.*
- Grade 2: *Presentation of Knowledge and Ideas 5. Create audio recordings of stories or poems; add drawings or other visual displays to stories or recounts of experiences when appropriate to clarify ideas, thoughts, and feelings.*

Demonstration Station – page 99

Kindergarten-Grade 3:
CCSS English Language Arts & Literacy: Language
- Kindergarten-Grade 1: *Vocabulary acquisition and Use 5. With guidance and support from adults, explore word relationships and nuances in word meanings. 5c. Identify real-life connections between words and their use (e.g., note places at school that are colorful… note places at home that are cozy).*
- Grades 2 & 3: *Vocabulary acquisition and Use 5. Demonstrate understanding of word relationships and nuances in word meanings. 5a. Identify real-life connections between words and their use (e.g., describe foods that are spicy or juicy … describe people who are friendly or helpful).*

Down to a System – page 100

Kindergarten-Grade 3:
CCSS English Language Arts & Literacy: Language
- Kindergarten-Grade 1: *Vocabulary acquisition and Use 5. With guidance and support from adults, explore word relationships and nuances in word meanings. 5a. Sort common objects into categories (e.g., shapes, foods ... colors, clothing ...) to gain a sense of the concepts the categories represent.*
- Grades 2 & 3: *Vocabulary acquisition and Use 5. Demonstrate understanding of word relationships and nuances in word meanings. 5a. Identify real-life connections between words and their use (e.g., describe foods that are spicy or juicy ... describe people who are friendly or helpful).*

Far, Far Away – page 101

Kindergarten-Grade 1:
CCSS English Language Arts & Literacy: Language
- Kindergarten: *Conventions of Standard English 1. Demonstrate command of the conventions of standard English grammar and usage when writing or speaking. 1a. Print many upper- and lowercase letters.*
- Grade 1: *Conventions of Standard English 1. Print all upper- and lowercase letters.*

Feeling Good! – page 102

Kindergarten-Grade 1
CCSS English Language Arts & Literacy: Language
- Kindergarten: *Conventions of Standard English 1. Demonstrate command of the conventions of standard English grammar and usage when writing or speaking. 1a. Print many upper- and lowercase letters.*
- Grade 1: *Conventions of Standard English 1. Print all upper- and lowercase letters.*

Not-a-Bore Chore – page 103

Kindergarten-Grade 3:
CCSS English Language Arts & Literacy: Language
- Kindergarten-Grade 1: *Vocabulary acquisition and Use 5. With guidance and support from adults, explore word relationships and nuances in word meanings.5a. Sort common objects into categories (e.g., shapes, foods ... colors, clothing ...) to gain a sense of the concepts the categories represent.*
- Grades 2 & 3: *Vocabulary acquisition and Use 5. Demonstrate understanding of word relationships and nuances in word meanings. 5a. Identify real-life connections between words and their use (e.g., describe foods that are spicy or juicy ... describe people who are friendly or helpful).*

Personal Speller – page 104

Kindergarten-Grade 5:
CCSS English Language Arts & Literacy: Language
- Kindergarten: *Conventions of Standard English 2d. Spell simple words phonetically, drawing on knowledge of sound-letter relationships.*
- Grade 1: *Conventions of Standard English 2d. Use conventional spelling for words with common spelling patterns and for frequently occurring irregular words. & 2e. Spell untaught words phonetically, drawing on phonemic awareness and spelling conventions.*
- Grade 2: *Conventions of Standard English 2e. Consult reference materials, including beginning dictionaries, as needed to check and correct spellings.*
- Grade 3: *Conventions of Standard English 2e. Use conventional spelling for high-frequency and other studied words and for adding suffixes to base words (e.g., sitting, smiled, cries, happiness). 2f. Use spelling patterns and generalizations (e.g., word families, position-based spellings, syllable patterns, ending rules, meaningful word parts) in writing words. 2g. Consult reference materials, including beginning dictionaries, as needed to check and correct spellings.*
- Grade 4 & 5: *Conventions of Standard English 2d (Gr. 4) 2e (Gr. 5). Spell grade-appropriate words correctly, consulting references as needed.*

Picture What You Mean! – page 105

Kindergarten-Grade 1:
CCSS English Language Arts & Literacy: *Language Vocabulary acquisition and Use 5. With guidance and support from adults, explore word relationships and nuances in word meanings. 5c. Identify real-life connections between words and their use (e.g., note places at school that are colorful; note places at home that are cozy).*

Rainbow Word Trace-Over – page 107

Kindergarten-Grade 1:
CCSS English Language Arts & Literacy: Language
- Kindergarten: *Conventions of Standard English 1. Demonstrate command of the conventions of standard English grammar and usage when writing or speaking. 1a. Print many upper- and lowercase letters.*
- Grade 1: *Conventions of Standard English 1. Print all upper- and lowercase letters.*

Sentence Scramble – page 108

Kindergarten-Grade 5:
CCSS English Language Arts & Literacy: Language
- Kindergarten: *Conventions of Standard English 1. Demonstrate command of the conventions of standard English grammar and usage when writing or speaking. 1f. Produce and expand complete sentences in shared language activities*

- Grade 1: *Conventions of Standard English 1. Demonstrate command of the conventions of standard English grammar and usage when writing or speaking. 1j. Produce and expand complete simple and compound declarative, interrogative, imperative, and exclamatory sentences in response to prompts.*
- Grade 2: *Conventions of Standard English 1. Demonstrate command of the conventions of standard English grammar and usage when writing or speaking. 1f. Produce, expand, and rearrange complete simple and compound sentences.*
- Grade 3: *Conventions of Standard English 1. Demonstrate command of the conventions of standard English grammar and usage when writing or speaking. 1i. Produce simple, compound, and complex sentences.*
- Grades 4-5: *Conventions of Standard English 1. Demonstrate command of the conventions of standard English grammar and usage when writing or speaking. 1f. Produce complete sentences, recognizing and correcting inappropriate fragments and run-ons....*

Shake It. Make It. – page 109

Kindergarten-Grade 5:
CCSS English Language Arts & Literacy: Language
- Kindergarten: *Conventions of Standard English 2d. Spell simple words phonetically, drawing on knowledge of sound-letter relationships.*
- Grade 1: *Conventions of Standard English 2d. Use conventional spelling for words with common spelling patterns and for frequently occurring irregular words. & 2e. Spell untaught words phonetically, drawing on phonemic awareness and spelling conventions.*
- Grade 2: *Conventions of Standard English 2e. Consult reference materials, including beginning dictionaries, as needed to check and correct spellings.*
- Grade 3: *Conventions of*

Standard English 2e. Use conventional spelling for high-frequency and other studied words and for adding suffixes to base words (e.g., sitting, smiled, cries, happiness). 2f. Use spelling pattern s and generalizations (e.g., word families, position-based spellings, syllable patterns, ending rules, meaningful word parts) in writing words. 2g. Consult reference materials, including beginning dictionaries, as needed to check and correct spellings.
- Grade 4 & 5: *Conventions of Standard English 2d (Gr. 4) 2e (Gr. 5). Spell grade-appropriate words correctly, consulting references as needed.*

Story Words – page 110

Kindergarten-Grade 3:
CCSS English Language Arts & Literacy: Language
- *Conventions of Standard English 1. Demonstrate command of the conventions of standard English grammar and usage when writing or speaking. 1b. (K) Use frequently occurring nouns and verbs; (Grade 1) Use common, proper, and possessive nouns; (Grade 2) Form and use frequently occurring irregular plural nouns (e.g., feet, children, teeth, mice, fish); (Grade 3) Form and use regular and irregular plural nouns.*

Taking Turns – page 111

Kindergarten-Grade 1:
CCSS English Language Arts & Literacy: Language
- Kindergarten: *Conventions of Standard English 1. Demonstrate command of the conventions of standard English grammar and usage when writing or speaking. 1f. Produce and expand complete sentences in shared language activities.*
- Grade 1: *Conventions of Standard English 1. Demonstrate command of the conventions of standard English grammar and usage when writing or speaking. 1j. Produce and expand complete simple and compound*

declarative, interrogative, imperative, and exclamatory sentences in response to prompts.

Kindergarten-Grade 3:
CCSS English Language Arts & Literacy: Speaking and Listening
- Kindergarten: *Presentation of Knowledge and Ideas 6. Speak audibly and express thoughts, feelings, and ideas clearly.*
- Grade 1: *Presentation of Knowledge and Ideas 6. Produce complete sentences when appropriate to task and situation.*
- Grade 2: *Presentation of Knowledge and Ideas 6. Produce complete sentences when appropriate to task and situation in order to provide requested detail or clarification.*
- Grade 3: *Presentation of Knowledge and Ideas 6. Speak in complete sentences when appropriate to task and situation in order to provide requested detail or clarification.*

The Right Fit – page 112

Kindergarten-Grade 1:
CCSS English Language Arts & Literacy: Language
- Kindergarten: *Conventions of Standard English 1. Demonstrate command of the conventions of standard English grammar and usage when writing or speaking. 1a. Print many upper- and lowercase letters.*
- Grade 1: *Conventions of Standard English 1. Print all upper- and lowercase letters.*

Thematic Picture Dictionary – page 113

Kindergarten-Grade 3:
CCSS English Language Arts & Literacy: Language
- Kindergarten-Grade 1: *Vocabulary acquisition and Use 5. With guidance and support from adults, explore word relationships and nuances in word meanings.*
- Grades 2 & 3: *Vocabulary acquisition and Use 5. Demonstrate understanding of word relationships and nuances in word meanings.*

Wish Lists – page 115

Kindergarten-Grade 3:

CCSS English Language Arts & Literacy: Language

- Kindergarten: *Vocabulary acquisition and Use 5. With guidance and support from adults, explore word relationships and nuances in word meanings. 5a Sort common objects into categories (e.g., shapes, foods) to gain a sense of the concepts the categories represent. 5c. Identify real-life connections between words and their use (e.g., note places at school that are colorful).*

- Grade 1: *Vocabulary acquisition and Use 5. With guidance and support from adults, explore word relationships and nuances in word meanings. 5a. Sort words into categories (e.g., colors, clothing) to gain a sense of the concepts the categories represent. and their use (e.g., describe foods that are spicy or juicy). 5b. Define words by category and by one or more key attributes (e.g., a duck is a bird that swims; a tiger is a large cat with stripes). 5c. Identify real-life connections between words and their use (e.g., note places at home that are cozy).*

- Grades 2: *Vocabulary acquisition and Use 5. Demonstrate understanding of word relationships and nuances in word meanings. 5a. Identify real-life connections between words and their use (e.g., describe foods that are spicy or juicy).*

- Grades 3: *Vocabulary acquisition and Use 5. Demonstrate understanding of word relationships and nuances in word meanings. 5a. Distinguish the literal and nonliteral meanings of words and phrases in context (e.g., take steps). 5b. Identify real life connections between words and their use (e.g., describe people who are friendly or helpful).*

Common Core State Standards

Reading Standards for Literature K-5 (RL) & Reading Standards for Informational Text K-5 (RI)

Common Core State Standards for English Language Arts & Literacy in History/Social Studies, Science, and Technical Subjects SOURCE: http://www.corestandards.org/assets/CCSSI_ELA%20 Standards.pdf (pages 10-14). © Copyright 2010. National Governors Association Center for Best Practices and Council of Chief State School Officers. All rights reserved.*

Reading Standards for Literature K-5 (RL) and Reading Standards for Informational Text K-5 (RI) offer a focus for instruction each year and help ensure that students gain adequate exposure to a range of texts and tasks. Rigor is also infused through the requirement that students read increasingly complex texts through the grades. Students advancing through the grades are expected to meet each year's grade-specific standards and retain or further develop skills and understandings mastered in preceding grades. (*Common Core Standards*, p. 11)

Reading: Literature and Informational Text

Before, During, and After – page 118

Kindergarten-Grade 5:
CCSS English Language Arts & Literacy: Reading Standards for Literature (RL) and Informational Text (RI)

- Kindergarten: *Key Ideas and details* 1. (RL & RI) *With prompting and support, ask and answer questions about key details in a text.* 2. (RL) *With prompting and support, retell familiar stories, including key details.* (RI) *With prompting and support, identify the main topic and retell key details of a text.* 3. (RL) *With prompting and support, identify characters, settings, and major events in a story.* (RI) *With prompting and support, describe the connection between two individuals, events, ideas, or pieces of information in a text.*

- Grade 1: *Key Ideas and details* 1. (RL & RI) *Ask and answer questions about key details in a text.* 2. (RL) *Retell stories, including key details, and demonstrate understanding of their central message or lesson.* (RI) *Identify the main topic and*

retell key details of a text. 3. (RL) *Describe characters, settings, and major events in a story, using key details.* (RI) *Describe the connection between two individuals, events, ideas, or pieces of information in a text.*

- Grade 2: *Key Ideas and details* 1. *Ask and answer such questions as who, what, where, when, why, and how to demonstrate understanding of key details in a text.* 2. (RL) *Recount stories, including fables and folktales from diverse cultures, and determine their central message, lesson, or moral.* (RI) *Identify the main topic of a multiparagraph text as well as the focus of specific paragraphs within the text.* 3. (RL) *Describe how characters in a story respond to major events and challenges.* (RI) *Describe the connection between a series of historical events, scientific ideas or concepts, or steps in technical procedures in a text.*

- Grade 3: *Key Ideas and details* 1. *Ask and answer questions to demonstrate understanding of a text, referring explicitly to the text as the basis for the answers.* 2. (RL) *Recount stories, including fables, folktales, and myths from diverse cultures; determine the*

central message, lesson, or moral and explain how it is conveyed through key details in the text. (RI) *Determine the main idea of a text; recount the key details and explain how they support the main idea.* 3. (RL) *Describe characters in a story (e.g., their traits, motivations, or feelings) and explain how their actions contribute to the sequence of events.* (RI) *Describe the relationship between a series of historical events, scientific ideas or concepts, or steps in technical procedures in a text, using language that pertains to time, sequence, and cause/effect.*

- Grade 4: *Key Ideas and details* 1. *Refer to details and examples in a text when explaining what the text says explicitly and when drawing inferences from the text.* 2. (RL) *Determine a theme of a story, drama, or poem from details in the text; summarize the text.* (RI) *Determine the main idea of a text and explain how it is supported by key details; summarize the text.* 3. (RL) *Describe in depth a character, setting, or event in a story or drama, drawing on specific details in the text (e.g., a character's thoughts, words, or actions).* (RI) *Explain events, procedures, ideas, or concepts in a historical, scientific, or technical text, including what happened and why, based on specific information in the text.*

- Grade 5: *Key Ideas and details. 1. Quote accurately from a text when explaining what the text says explicitly and when drawing inferences from the text. 2. (RL) Determine a theme of a story, drama, or poem from details in the text, including how characters in a story or drama respond to challenges or how the speaker in a poem reflects upon a topic; summarize the text. (RI) Determine two or more main ideas of a text and explain how they are supported by key details; summarize the text. 3. (RL) Compare and contrast two or more characters, settings, or events in a story or drama, drawing on specific details in the text (e.g., how characters interact). (RI) Explain the relationships or interactions between two or more individuals, events, ideas, or concepts in a historical, scientific, or technical text based on specific information in the text.*

Go and Know – page 119

Kindergarten–Grade 5:
CCSS English Language Arts & Literacy: Reading Standards for Informational Text (RI)

- Kindergarten: *Key Ideas and details 1. (RI) With prompting and support, ask and answer questions about key details in a text. 2. (RI) With prompting and support, identify the main topic and retell key details of a text.*
- Grade 1: *Key Ideas and details 1. (RI) Ask and answer questions about key details in a text. 2. (RI) Identify the main topic and retell key details of a text.*
- Grade 2: *Key Ideas and details 1. Ask and answer such questions as who, what, where, when, why, and how to demonstrate understanding of key details in a text. 2. (RI) Identify the main topic of a multiparagraph text as well as the focus of specific*

paragraphs within the text.

- Grade 3: *Key Ideas and details 1. Ask and answer questions to demonstrate understanding of a text, referring explicitly to the text as the basis for the answers. 2. (RI) Determine the main idea of a text; recount the key details and explain how they support the main idea.*
- Grade 4: *Key Ideas and details 1. Refer to details and examples in a text when explaining what the text says explicitly and when drawing inferences from the text. 2. (RI) Determine the main idea of a text and explain how it is supported by key details; summarize the text.*
- Grade 5: *Key Ideas and details. 1. Quote accurately from a text when explaining what the text says explicitly and when drawing inferences from the text. 2. (RI) Determine two or more main ideas of a text and explain how they are supported by key details; summarize the text.*

I Can Read It and Do It – page 122

Grades 3–5:
CCSS English Language Arts & Literacy: Reading Standards for Informational Text (RI)

- Grade 3: *Integration of Knowledge and Ideas 7. (RI) Use information gained from illustrations (e.g., maps, photographs) and the words in a text to demonstrate understanding of the text (e.g., where, when, why, and how key events occur).*
- Grade 4: *Integration of Knowledge and Ideas 7. (RI) Interpret information presented visually, orally, or quantitatively (e.g., in charts, graphs, diagrams, time lines, animations, or interactive elements on Web pages) and explain how the information contributes to an understanding of the text in which it appears.*
- Grade 5: *Integration of Knowledge and Ideas 7. (RI) Draw on information from multiple print or digital sources, demonstrating the ability to*

locate an answer to a question quickly or to solve a problem efficiently.

It's Fun to Organize – page 123

Kindergarten–Grade 5:
CCSS English Language Arts & Literacy: Reading Standards for Literature (RL)

- Kindergarten: *Key Ideas and details 3. (RL) With prompting and support, identify characters, settings, and major events in a story.*
- Grade 1: *Key Ideas and details 3. (RL) Describe characters, settings, and major events in a story, using key details.*
- Grade 2: *Key Ideas and details 3. (RL) Describe how characters in a story respond to major events and challenges.*
- Grade 3: *Key Ideas and details 3. (RL) Describe characters in a story (e.g., their traits, motivations, or feelings) and explain how their actions contribute to the sequence of events.*
- Grade 4: *Key Ideas and details 3. (RL) Describe in depth a character, setting, or event in a story or drama, drawing on specific details in the text (e.g., a character's thoughts, words, or actions).*
- Grade 5: *Key Ideas and details 3. (RL) Compare and contrast two or more characters, settings, or events in a story or drama, drawing on specific details in the text (e.g., how characters interact).*

Grades 2–5:
CCSS English Language Arts & Literacy: Reading Standards for Literature (RL)

- Grades 2-3: *Range of Reading and Level of Text Complexity 10. By the end of the year, read and comprehend literature, including stories and poetry, in the grades 2–3 text complexity band proficiently, with scaffolding as needed at the high end of the range.*
- Grades 4-5: *Range of Reading and Level of Text Complexity 10. By the end of the year, read and*

comprehend literature,including stories, dramas, and poetry, at the high end of the grades 4–5 text complexity band independently and proficiently.

Laugh It Up – page 126

Kindergarten–Grade 5:

CCSS English Language Arts & Literacy: Reading Standards for Literature (RL)

- Kindergarten: *Key Ideas and details 2. (RL) With prompting and support, retell familiar stories, including key details.*
- Grade 1: *Key Ideas and details 2. (RL) Retell stories, including key details, and demonstrate understanding of their central message or lesson.*
- Grade 2: *Key Ideas and details 2. (RL) Recount stories, including fables and folktales from diverse cultures, and determine their central message, lesson, or moral.*
- Grade 3: *Key Ideas and details 2. (RL) Recount stories, including fables, folktales, and myths from diverse cultures; determine the central message, lesson, or moral and explain how it is conveyed through key details in the text.*
- Grade 4: *Key Ideas and details 2. (RL) Determine a theme of a story, drama, or poem from details in the text; summarize the text.*
- Grade 5: *Key Ideas and details. 2. (RL) Determine a theme of a story, drama, or poem from details in the text, including how characters in a story or drama respond to challenges or how the speaker in a poem reflects upon a topic; summarize the text.*

Picture It – page 127

Kindergarten–Grade 5:

CCSS English Language Arts & Literacy: Reading Standards for Literature (RL) and Informational Text (RI)

- Kindergarten: *Integration of Knowledge and Ideas 7. (RL) With prompting and support, describe the relationship between illustrations and the story in which they appear (e.g., what moment in a story an illustration depicts). (RI) With prompting and support, describe the relationship between illustrations and the text in which they appear (e.g., what person, place, thing, or idea in the text an illustration depicts).*
- Grade 1: *Integration of Knowledge and Ideas 7. (RL) Use illustrations and details in a story to describe its characters, setting, or events. (RI) Use the illustrations and details in a text to describe its key ideas.*
- Grade 2: *Integration of Knowledge and Ideas 7. (RL) Use information gained from the illustrations and words in a print or digital text to demonstrate understanding of its characters, setting, or plot. (RI) Explain how specific images (e.g., a diagram showing how a machine works) contribute to and clarify a text.*
- Grade 3: *Integration of Knowledge and Ideas 7. (RL) Explain how specific aspects of a text's illustrations contribute to what is conveyed by the words in a story (e.g., create mood, emphasize aspects of a character or setting). (RI) Use information gained from illustrations (e.g., maps, photographs) and the words in a text to demonstrate understanding of the text (e.g., where, when, why, and how key events occur).*
- Grade 4: *Integration of Knowledge and Ideas 7. (RL) Make connections between the text of a story or drama and a visual or oral presentation of the text, identifying where each version reflects specific descriptions and directions in the text. (RI) Interpret information presented visually, orally, or quantitatively (e.g., in charts, graphs, diagrams, time lines, animations, or interactive elements on Web pages) and explain how the information contributes to an understanding of the text in which it appears.*
- Grade 5: *Integration of Knowledge and Ideas 7. (RL) Analyze how visual and multimedia elements contribute to the meaning, tone, or beauty of a text (e.g., graphic novel, multimedia presentation of fiction, folktale, myth, poem). (RI) Draw on information from multiple print or digital sources, demonstrating the ability to locate an answer to a question quickly or to solve a problem efficiently.*

Positive Role Models – page 128

Kindergarten–Grade 5:

CCSS English Language Arts & Literacy: Reading Standards for Informational Text (RI)

- Kindergarten: *Key Ideas and details 1. With prompting and support, ask and answer questions about key details in a text. 2. (RI) With prompting and support, identify the main topic and retell key details of a text. 3. (RI) With prompting and support, describe the connection between two individuals, events, ideas, or pieces of information in a text.*
- Grade 1: *Key Ideas and details 1. Ask and answer questions about key details in a text. 2. (RI) Identify the main topic and retell key details of a text. 3. (RI) Describe the connection between two individuals, events, ideas, or pieces of information in a text.*
- Grade 2: *Key Ideas and details 1. Ask and answer such questions as who, what, where, when, why, and how to demonstrate understanding of key details in a text. 2. (RI) Identify the main topic of a multiparagraph text as well as the focus of specific paragraphs within the text. 3. (RI) Describe the connection between a series of historical events, scientific ideas or concepts, or steps in technical procedures in a text.*
- Grade 3: *Key Ideas and details 1. Ask and answer questions to demonstrate understanding of a text, referring explicitly to the text as the basis for the answers. 2. (RI) Determine the main idea of a text; recount the key details and explain how they support the main idea. 3. (RI) Describe the relationship between a series of historical events, scientific ideas or concepts, or steps in technical*

procedures in a text, using language that pertains to time, sequence, and cause/effect.

- Grade 4: *Key Ideas and details 1. Refer to details and examples in a text when explaining what the text says explicitly and when drawing inferences from the text. 2. (RI) Determine the main idea of a text and explain how it is supported by key details; summarize the text. 3. (RI) Explain events, procedures, ideas, or concepts in a historical, scientific, or technical text, including what happened and why, based on specific information in the text.*
- Grade 5: *Key Ideas and details. 1. Quote accurately from a text when explaining what the text says explicitly and when drawing inferences from the text. 2. (RI) Determine two or more main ideas of a text and explain how they are supported by key details; summarize the text. 3. (RI) Explain the relationships or interactions between two or more individuals, events, ideas, or concepts in a historical, scientific, or technical text based on specific information in the text.*

Reading All Around – page 129

Kindergarten-Grade 5:
CCSS English Language Arts & Literacy: Reading Standards for Literature (RL) and Informational Text (RI)

- Kindergarten: *Range of Reading and Level of Text Complexity 10. (RL & RI) Actively engage in group reading activities with purpose and understanding.*
- Grade 1: *Range of Reading and Level of Text Complexity 10. (RL) With prompting and support, read prose and poetry of appropriate complexity for grade 1. (RI) With prompting and support, read informational texts appropriately complex for grade 1.*
- Grades 2-3: *Range of Reading and Level of Text Complexity 10. (RL) By the end of the year, read and comprehend literature,*

including stories and poetry, in the grades 2–3 text complexity band proficiently, with scaffolding as needed at the high end of the range. (RI) By the end of year, read and comprehend informational texts, including history/social studies, science, and technical texts, in the grades 2–3 text complexity band proficiently, with scaffolding as needed at the high end of the range.

- Grades 4-5: *Range of Reading and Level of Text Complexity 10. (RL) By the end of the year, read and comprehend literature, including stories, dramas, and poetry, at the high end of the grades 4–5 text complexity band independently and proficiently. (RI) By the end of the year, read and comprehend informational texts, including history/social studies, science, and technical texts, at the high end of the grades 4–5 text complexity band independently and proficiently.*

Reading Is Everywhere! – page 130

Kindergarten-Grade 5:
CCSS English Language Arts & Literacy: Reading Standards for Literature (RL)

- Kindergarten: *Key Ideas and details 2. (RL) With prompting and support, retell familiar stories, including key details.*
- Grade 1: *Key Ideas and details 2. (RL) Retell stories, including key details, and demonstrate understanding of their central message or lesson.*
- Grade 2: *Key Ideas and details 2. (RL) Recount stories, including fables and folktales from diverse cultures, and determine their central message, lesson, or moral.*
- Grade 3: *Key Ideas and details 2. (RL) Recount stories, including fables, folktales, and myths from diverse cultures; determine the central message, lesson, or moral and explain how it is conveyed through key details in the text.*
- Grade 4: *Key Ideas and details 2.(RL) Determine a theme of a story, drama, or poem from details in the text; summarize the text.*

- Grade 5: *Key Ideas and details. 2. (RL) Determine a theme of a story, drama, or poem from details in the text, including how characters in a story or drama respond to challenges or how the speaker in a poem reflects upon a topic; summarize the text.*

Show It When You Know It – page 131

Kindergarten-Grade 5:
CCSS English Language Arts & Literacy: Reading Standards for Literature (RL)

- Kindergarten: *Key Ideas and details 2. (RL) With prompting and support, retell familiar stories, including key details.*
- Grade 1: *Key Ideas and details 2. (RL) Retell stories, including key details, and demonstrate understanding of their central message or lesson.*
- Grade 2: *Key Ideas and details 2. (RL) Recount stories, including fables and folktales from diverse cultures, and determine their central message, lesson, or moral.*
- Grade 3: *Key Ideas and details 2. (RL) Recount stories, including fables, folktales, and myths from diverse cultures; determine the central message, lesson, or moral and explain how it is conveyed through key details in the text.*
- Grade 4: *Key Ideas and details 2. (RL) Determine a theme of a story, drama, or poem from details in the text; summarize the text.*
- Grade 5: *Key Ideas and details. 2. (RL) Determine a theme of a story, drama, or poem from details in the text, including how characters in a story or drama respond to challenges or how the speaker in a poem reflects upon a topic; summarize the text.*

Kindergarten-Grade 5:
CCSS English Language Arts & Literacy: Speaking and Listening

- Grade K: *Presentation of Knowledge and Ideas 5. Add drawings or other visual displays to descriptions as desired to provide additional detail.*

- Grade 1: *Presentation of Knowledge and Ideas 5. Add drawings or other visual displays to descriptions when appropriate to clarify ideas, thoughts, and feelings.*
- Grade 2: *Presentation of Knowledge and Ideas 5. Create audio recordings of stories or poems; add drawings or other visual displays to stories or recounts of experiences when appropriate to clarify ideas, thoughts, and feelings.*
- Grade 3: *Presentation of Knowledge and Ideas 5. Create engaging audio recordings of stories or poems that demonstrate fluid reading at an understandable pace; add visual displays when appropriate to emphasize or enhance certain facts or details.*
- Grade 4: *Presentation of Knowledge and Ideas 5. Add audio recordings and visual displays to presentations when appropriate to enhance the development of main ideas or themes.*
- Grade 5: *Presentation of Knowledge and Ideas 5. Include multimedia components (e.g., graphics, sound) and visual displays in presentations when appropriate to enhance the development of main ideas or themes.*

Stump the Grown-Up – page 132

Kindergarten-Grade 3:
CCSS English Language Arts & Literacy: Reading Standards for Literature (RL) and Informational Text (RI)
- Kindergarten: *Key Ideas and details 1. (RL & RI) With prompting and support, ask and answer questions about key details in a text.*
- Grade 1: *Key Ideas and details 1. (RL & RI) Ask and answer questions about key details in a text.*
- Grade 2: *Key Ideas and details 1. Ask and answer such questions as who, what, where, when, why, and how to demonstrate understanding of key details in a text.*

- Grade 3: *Key Ideas and details 1. Ask and answer questions to demonstrate understanding of a text, referring explicitly to the text as the basis for the answers.*
- Grade 4: *Key Ideas and details 1. Refer to details and examples in a text when explaining what the text says explicitly and when drawing inferences from the text.*
- Grade 5: *Key Ideas and details. 1. Quote accurately from a text when explaining what the text says explicitly and when drawing inferences from the text.*

Kindergarten-Grade 2:
CCSS English Language Arts & Literacy: *Speaking and Listening*
- Kindergarten: *Comprehension and Collaboration 2. Confirm understanding of a text read aloud or information presented orally or through other media by asking and answering questions about key details and requesting clarification if something is not understood.*
- Grades 1-2: *Comprehension and Collaboration 2. Ask and answer questions about key details in a text read aloud or information presented orally or through other media.*

Take a Wild Guess – page 133

Kindergarten-Grade 5:
CCSS English Language Arts & Literacy: Reading Standards for Literature (RL) and Informational Text (RI)
- Kindergarten: *Key Ideas and details 1. (RL & RI) With prompting and support, ask and answer questions about key details in a text. 2. (RL) With prompting and support, retell familiar stories, including key details. (RI) With prompting and support, identify the main topic and retell key details of a text. 3. (RL) With prompting and support, identify characters, settings, and major events in a story. (RI) With prompting and support, describe the connection between two individuals, events, ideas, or pieces of information in a text.*

- Grade 1: *Key Ideas and details 1. (RL & RI) Ask and answer questions about key details in a text. 2. (RL) Retell stories, including key details, and demonstrate understanding of their central message or lesson. (RI) Identify the main topic and retell key details of a text. 3. (RL) Describe characters, settings, and major events in a story, using key details. (RI) Describe the connection between two individuals, events, ideas, or pieces of information in a text.*
- Grade 2: *Key Ideas and details 1. Ask and answer such questions as who, what, where, when, why, and how to demonstrate understanding of key details in a text. 2. (RL) Recount stories, including fables and folktales from diverse cultures, and determine their central message, lesson, or moral. 3. (RL) Describe how characters in a story respond to major events and challenges.*
- Grade 3: *Key Ideas and details 1. Ask and answer questions to demonstrate understanding of a text, referring explicitly to the text as the basis for the answers. 2. (RL) Recount stories, including fables, folktales, and myths from diverse cultures; determine the central message, lesson, or moral and explain how it is conveyed through key details in the text. 3. (RL) Describe characters in a story (e.g., their traits, motivations, or feelings) and explain how their actions contribute to the sequence of events.*
- Grade 4: *Key Ideas and details 1. Refer to details and examples in a text when explaining what the text says explicitly and when drawing inferences from the text. 2. (RL) Determine a theme of a story, drama, or poem from details in the text; summarize the text. 3. (RL) Describe in depth a character, setting, or event in a story or drama, drawing on specific details in the text (e.g., a character's thoughts, words, or actions).*

- Grade 5: *Key Ideas and details. 1. Quote accurately from a text when explaining what the text says explicitly and when drawing inferences from the text. 2. (RL) Determine a theme of a story, drama, or poem from details in the text, including how characters in a story or drama respond to challenges or how the speaker in a poem reflects upon a topic; summarize the text. 3. (RL) Compare and contrast two or more characters, settings, or events in a story or drama, drawing on specific details in the text (e.g., how characters interact).*

Common Core State Standards

Writing Standards K-5 (W)

Common Core State Standards for English Language Arts & Literacy in History/Social Studies, Science, and Technical Subjects
SOURCE: http://www.corestandards.org/assets/CCSSI_ELA%20Standards.pdf (Pages 18–21).
© Copyright 2010. National Governors Association Center for Best Practices and Council of Chief State School Officers. All rights reserved.*

Writing standards for K–5 offer a focus for instruction each year to help ensure that students gain adequate mastery of a range of skills and applications. Each year in their writing, students should demonstrate increasing sophistication in all aspects of language use, from vocabulary and syntax to the development and organization of ideas, and they should address increasingly demanding content and sources.

Students advancing through the grades are expected to meet each year's grade-specific standards and retain or further develop skills and understandings mastered in preceding grades. The expected growth in student writing ability is reflected both in the standards themselves and in the collection of annotated student writing samples … (*Common Core State Standards*, p. 19)

Writing

A Special Place – page 136

Grades K-5
CCSS English Language Arts & Literacy: Writing Standards
- Kinergarten: *5. With guidance and support from adults, respond to questions and suggestions from peers and add details to strengthen writing as needed.*
- Grade 1: *5. With guidance and support from adults, focus on a topic, respond to questions and suggestions from peers, and add details to strengthen writing as needed.*
- Grades 2-5 Writing Standards: Production and distribution of Writing 5. *With guidance and support from peers and adults, develop and strengthen writing as needed by planning, revising, and editing.*

Be on the Lookout – page 137

Kindergarten-Grade 5
CCSS English Language Arts & Literacy: Writing Standards-*Text Types and Purpose.*
- Kindergarten: *Use a combination of drawing, dictating, and writing to compose opinion pieces in which they tell a reader the topic or the name of the book they are writing about and state an opinion or preference about the topic or book.*
- Grades 1-2: *Write opinion pieces in which they introduce the topic or name the book they are writing about.*
- Grades 3-5 1. *Write opinion pieces on topics or texts, supporting a point of view with reasons*
- Grade 1: *Text Types and Purposes 2. Write informative/explanatory texts in which they name a topic, supply some facts about the topic, and provide some sense of closure. 3. Write narratives in which they recount two or more appropriately sequenced events, include some details regarding what happened, use temporal words to signal event order, and provide some sense of closure.*
- Grade 2: *Text Types and Purposes 2. Write informative/explanatory texts in which they introduce a topic, use facts and definitions to develop points, and provide a concluding statement or section. 3. Write narratives in which they recount a well-elaborated event or short sequence of events, include details to describe actions, thoughts, and feelings, use temporal words to signal event order, and provide a sense of closure.*
- Grades 3-5: *Text Types and Purposes 2. Write informative/explanatory texts to examine a topic and convey ideas and information clearly. 3. Write narratives to develop real or imagined experiences or events using effective technique, descriptive details, and clear event sequences*

Break It Up – page 138

Kindergarten-Grade 5
CCSS English Language Arts & Literacy: Writing Standards
- Kindergarten: *Text Types and Purposes 3. Use a combination of drawing, dictating, and writing to narrate a single event or several loosely linked events, tell about the events in the order in which they occurred, and provide a reaction to what happened.*
- Grade 1: *Text Types and Purposes 3. Write narratives in which they recount two or more*

appropriately sequenced events, include some details regarding what happened, use temporal words to signal event order, and provide some sense of closure.

- Grade 2: *Text Types and Purposes 3. Write narratives in which they recount a well-elaborated event or short sequence of events, include details to describe actions, thoughts, and feelings, use temporal words to signal event order, and provide a sense of closure.*
- Grades 3-5: *Text Types and Purposes 3. Write narratives to develop real or imagined experiences or events using effective technique, descriptive details, and clear event sequences.*

Create a Caption – page 139

Kindergarten:
CCSS English Language Arts & Literacy: Writing Standards

- Kindergarten: *Text Types and Purposes 2. Use a combination of drawing, dictating, and writing to compose informative/ explanatory texts in which they name what they are writing about and supply some information about the topic. 3. Use a combination of drawing, dictating, and writing to narrate a single event or several loosely linked events, tell about the events in the order in which they occurred, and provide a reaction to what happened.*

Grade 2:
CCSS English Language Arts & Literacy: Reading Standards for Informational Text

- *Craft and Structure 5. Know and use various text features (e.g., captions, bold print, subheadings, glossaries, indexes, electronic menus, icons) to locate key facts or information in a text efficiently.*

Gifts for Writing Fun! – page 140

Kindergarten-Grade 5
CCSS English Language Arts & Literacy: Writing Standards

- Kindergarten: *Text Types and Purposes 3. Use a combination of*

drawing, dictating, and writing to narrate a single event or several loosely linked events, tell about the events in the order in which they occurred, and provide a reaction to what happened.

- Grades 1-2: *Text Types and Purposes 3. Write narratives in which they recount two or more appropriately sequenced events, include some details regarding what happened, use temporal words to signal event order, and provide some sense of closure.*
- Grades 3-5: *Text Types and Purposes 3. Write narratives to develop real or imagined experiences or events using effective technique, descriptive details, and clear event sequences.*

Good-Work Meeting Day – page 141

Kindergarten-Grade 5
CCSS English Language Arts & Literacy: Writing Standards

- Kindergarten-Grade 1: *Research to Build and Present Knowledge 8. With guidance and support from adults, recall information from experiences or gather information from provided sources to answer a question.*
- Grade 2: *Research to Build and Present Knowledge 8. Recall information from experiences or gather information from provided sources to answer a question.*
- Grade 3: *Research to Build and Present Knowledge 8. Recall information from experiences or gather information from print and digital sources; take brief notes on sources and sort evidence into provided categories.*
- Grades 4 & 5: *Research to Build and Present Knowledge 8. Recall relevant information from experiences or gather relevant information from print and digital sources; take notes and categorize information, and provide a list of sources.*

Less May Be Best – page 142

Kindergarten-Grade 5
CCSS English Language Arts & Literacy: Writing Standards

- Kindergarten: *Text Types and Purposes 3. Use a combination of drawing, dictating, and writing to narrate a single event or several loosely linked events, tell about the events in the order in which they occurred, and provide a reaction to what happened.*
- Grade 1: *Text Types and Purposes 3. Write narratives in which they recount two or more appropriately sequenced events, include some details regarding what happened, use temporal words to signal event order, and provide some sense of closure.*
- Grade 2: *Text Types and Purposes 3. Write narratives in which they recount a well-elaborated event or short sequence of events, include details to describe actions, thoughts, and feelings, use temporal words to signal event order, and provide a sense of closure.*
- Grades 3-5: *Text Types and Purposes 3. Write narratives to develop real or imagined experiences or events using effective technique, descriptive details, and clear event sequences.*

Letter-Message Guide – page 144

Kindergarten-Grade 4
CCSS English Language Arts & Literacy: Writing Standards

- Kindergarten-Grade 2: *Production and distribution of Writing 6. With guidance and support from adults, use a variety of digital tools to produce and publish writing, including in collaboration with peers.*
- Grade 3: *Production and distribution of Writing 6. With guidance and support from adults, use technology to produce and publish writing (using keyboarding skills) as well as to interact and collaborate with others.*
- Grade 4: *Production and distribution of Writing 6. With some guidance and support from adults, use technology, including the Internet, to produce and publish writing as well as to interact and collaborate with others; demonstrate sufficient*

command of keyboarding skills to type a minimum of one page in a single sitting.

- Grade 5: *Production and distribution of Writing 6. With some guidance and support from adults, use technology, including the Internet, to produce and publish writing as well as to interact and collaborate with others; demonstrate sufficient command of keyboarding skills to type a minimum of two pages in a single sitting.*

Grades 3-5
CCSS English Language Arts & Literacy: Writing Standards
- *Range of Writing 10. Write routinely over extended time frames (time for research, reflection, and revision) and shorter time frames (a single sitting or a day or two) for a range of discipline-specific tasks, purposes, and audiences.*

My Daily Schedule – page 145

Kindergarten-Grade 5
- Kindergarten: *Text Types and Purposes- Use a combination of drawing, dictating, and writing to narrate a single event or several loosely linked events, tell about the events in the order in which they occurred, and provide a reaction to what happened.*
- Grade 1: *Text Types and Purposes - Write narratives in which they recount two or more appropriately sequenced events, include some details regarding what happened, use temporal words to signal event order, and provide some sense of closure.*
- Grade 2: *Text Types and Purposes - Write narratives in which they recount a well-elaborated event or short sequence of events, include details to describe actions, thoughts, and feelings, use temporal words to signal event order, and provide a sense of closure.*
- Grades 3–5: *Text Types and Purposes - Write narratives to develop real or imagined experiences or events using effective technique, descriptive details, and clear event sequences.*

No Boundaries – page 146

Kindergarten-Grade 1:
CCSS English Language Arts & Literacy:
- Kindergarten: *Conventions of Standard English 1. Demonstrate command of the conventions of standard English grammar and usage when writing or speaking. 1a. Print many upper- and lowercase letters.*
- Grade 1: *Conventions of Standard English 1. Print all upper- and lowercase letters.*

Notice the "Good Stuff" – page 147

Kindergarten-Grade 5
CCSS English Language Arts & Literacy: Writing Standards
- Kindergarten: *Production and distribution of Writing 5. With guidance and support from adults, respond to questions and suggestions from peers and add details to strengthen writing as needed.*
- Grade 1: *Production and distribution of Writing 5. With guidance and support from adults, focus on a topic, respond to questions and suggestions from peers, and add details to strengthen writing as needed.*
- Grade 2: *Production and distribution of Writing 5. With guidance and support from adults and peers, focus on a topic and strengthen writing as needed by revising and editing.*
- Grades 3 & 4: *Production and distribution of Writing 5. With guidance and support from peers and adults, develop and strengthen writing as needed by planning, revising, and editing.*
- Grade 5: *Production and distribution of Writing 5. With guidance and support from peers and adults, develop and strengthen writing as needed by planning, revising, editing, rewriting, or trying a new approach.*

Perfect Pen Pals – page 148

Kindergarten-Grade 5
CCSS English Language Arts & Literacy: Writing Standards

- Kindergarten-Grade 2: *Production and distribution of Writing 6. With guidance and support from adults, use a variety of digital tools to produce and publish writing, including in collaboration with peers.*
- Grade 3: *Production and distribution of Writing 6. With guidance and support from adults, use technology to produce and publish writing (using keyboarding skills) as well as to interact and collaborate with others.*
- Grade 4: *Production and distribution of Writing 6. With some guidance and support from adults, use technology, including the Internet, to produce and publish writing as well as to interact and collaborate with others; demonstrate sufficient command of keyboarding skills to type a minimum of one page in a single sitting.*
- Grade 5: *Production and distribution of Writing 6. With some guidance and support from adults, use technology, including the Internet, to produce and publish writing as well as to interact and collaborate with others; demonstrate sufficient command of keyboarding skills to type a minimum of two pages in a single sitting.*

Playing Secretary – page 149

Reading Standards: Foundational Skills - Print Concepts
Kindergarten-Grade 1: 1. Demonstrate understanding of the organization and basic features of print.
Kindergarten - b. Recognize that spoken words are represented in written language by specific sequences of letters.
Grade 1: a. Recognize the distinguishing features of a sentence (e.g., first word, capitalization, ending punctuation).

Kindergarten-Grade 4
CCSS English Language Arts & Literacy: Writing Standards
- Kindergarten: *Text Types and*

Purposes 1. Use a combination of drawing, dictating, and writing to compose opinion pieces in which they tell a reader the topic or the name of the book they are writing about and state an opinion or preference about the topic or book (e.g., My favorite book is ...). 2. Use a combination of drawing, dictating, and writing to compose informative/ explanatory texts in which they name what they are writing about and supply some information about the topic. 3. Use a combination of drawing, dictating, and writing to narrate a single event or several loosely linked events, tell about the events in the order in which they occurred, and provide a reaction to what happened.

See Writing Grow – page 150

Kindergarten-Grade 5
CCSS English Language Arts & Literacy: Writing Standards
- Kindergarten: *Text Types and Purposes 3. Use a combination of drawing, dictating, and writing to narrate a single event or several loosely linked events, tell about the events in the order in which they occurred, and provide a reaction to what happened.*
- Grade 1: *Text Types and Purposes 3. Write narratives in which they recount two or more appropriately sequenced events, include some details regarding what happened, use temporal words to signal event order, and provide some sense of closure.*
- Grade 2: *Text Types and Purposes 3. Write narratives in which they recount a well-elaborated event or short sequence of events, include details to describe actions, thoughts, and feelings, use temporal words to signal event order, and provide a sense of closure.*
- Grades 3-5: *Text Types and Purposes 3. Write narratives to develop real or imagined experiences or events using effective technique, descriptive details, and clear event sequences.*

Kindergarten-Grade 2:
CCSS English Language Arts & Literacy: Speaking and Listening
- Grade K: *Presentation of Knowledge and Ideas 5. Add drawings or other visual displays to descriptions as desired to provide additional detail.*
- Grade 1: *Presentation of Knowledge and Ideas 5. Add drawings or other visual displays to descriptions when appropriate to clarify ideas, thoughts, and feelings.*
- Grade 2: *Presentation of Knowledge and Ideas 5. Create audio recordings of stories or poems; add drawings or other visual displays to stories or recounts of experiences when appropriate to clarify ideas, thoughts, and feelings.*

Sloppy Copy – page 152

Kindergarten-Grade 5
CCSS English Language Arts & Literacy: Writing Standards
- Kindergarten: *Production and distribution of Writing 5. With guidance and support from adults, respond to questions and suggestions from peers and add details to strengthen writing as needed.*
- Grade 1: *Production and distribution of Writing 5. With guidance and support from adults, focus on a topic, respond to questions and suggestions from peers, and add details to strengthen writing as needed.*
- Grade 2: *Production and distribution of Writing 5. With guidance and support from adults and peers, focus on a topic and strengthen writing as needed by revising and editing.*
- Grades 3 & 4: *Production and distribution of Writing 5. With guidance and support from peers and adults, develop and strengthen writing as needed by planning, revising, and editing.*
- Grade 5: *Production and distribution of Writing 5. With guidance and support from peers and adults, develop and strengthen writing as needed by planning, revising, editing, rewriting, or trying a new approach.*

The Writing Process – page 153

Kindergarten-Grade 5
CCSS English Language Arts & Literacy: Writing Standards
- Kindergarten: *Production and distribution of Writing 5. With guidance and support from adults, respond to questions and suggestions from peers and add details to strengthen writing as needed.*
- Grade 1: *Production and distribution of Writing 5. With guidance and support from adults, focus on a topic, respond to questions and suggestions from peers, and add details to strengthen writing as needed.*
- Grade 2: *Production and distribution of Writing 5. With guidance and support from adults and peers, focus on a topic and strengthen writing as needed by revising and editing.*
- Grades 3 & 4: *Production and distribution of Writing 5. With guidance and support from peers and adults, develop and strengthen writing as needed by planning, revising, and editing.*
- Grade 5: *Production and distribution of Writing 5. With guidance and support from peers and adults, develop and strengthen writing as needed by planning, revising, editing, rewriting, or trying a new approach.*

Kindergarten-Grade 5
CCSS English Language Arts & Literacy: Writing Standards
- Kindergarten-Grade 2: *Production and distribution of Writing 6. With guidance and support from adults, use a variety of digital tools to produce and publish writing, including in collaboration with peers.*
- Grade 3: *Production and distribution of Writing 6. With guidance and support from adults, use technology to produce and publish writing (using keyboarding skills) as well as to interact and collaborate with others.*
- Grade 4: *Production and distribution of Writing 6. With some guidance and support from*

adults, use technology, including the Internet, to produce and publish writing as well as to interact and collaborate with others; demonstrate sufficient command of keyboarding skills to type a minimum of one page in a single sitting.
- Grade 5: *Production and distribution of Writing 6. With some guidance and support from adults, use technology, including the Internet, to produce and publish writing as well as to interact and collaborate with others; demonstrate sufficient command of keyboarding skills to type a minimum of two pages in a single sitting.*

To-Do Lists – page 154

Kindergarten-Grade 5
CCSS English Language Arts & Literacy: Writing Standards
- Kindergarten: *Text Types and Purposes 3. Use a combination of drawing, dictating, and writing to narrate a single event or several loosely linked events, tell about the events in the order in which they occurred, and provide a reaction to what happened.*
- Grade 1: *Text Types and Purposes 3. Write narratives in which they recount two or more appropriately sequenced events, include some details regarding what happened, use temporal words to signal event order, and provide some sense of closure.*
- Grade 2: *Text Types and Purposes 3. Write narratives in which they recount a well-elaborated event or short sequence of events, include details to describe actions, thoughts, and feelings, use temporal words to signal event order, and provide a sense of closure.*
- Grades 3-5: *Text Types and Purposes 3. Write narratives to develop real or imagined*

experiences or events using effective technique, descriptive details, and clear event sequences.

Turn It Around – page 155

Kindergarten-Grade 1:
CCSS English Language Arts & Literacy: Language
- Kindergarten: *Conventions of Standard English 1. Demonstrate command of the conventions of standard English grammar and usage when writing or speaking. 1a. Print many upper- and lowercase letters.*
- Grade 1: *Conventions of Standard English 1. Print all upper- and lowercase letters.*

Why Read and Write? – page 156

Kindergarten-Grade 5
CCSS English Language Arts & Literacy: Writing Standards
- Kindergarten-Grade 1: *Research to Build and Present Knowledge 8. With guidance and support from adults, recall information from experiences or gather information from provided sources to answer a question.*
- Grade 2: *Research to Build and Present Knowledge 8. Recall information from experiences or gather information from provided sources to answer a question.*
- Grade 3: *Research to Build and Present Knowledge 8. Recall information from experiences or gather information from print and digital sources; take brief notes on sources and sort evidence into provided categories.*
- Grades 4 & 5: *Research to Build and Present Knowledge 8. Recall relevant information from experiences or gather relevant information from print and digital sources; take notes and categorize information, and provide a list of sources.*

Write Away – page 158

Grades 3-5
CCSS English Language Arts & Literacy: Writing Standards
- *Range of Writing 10. Write routinely over extended time frames (time for research, reflection, and revision) and shorter time frames (a single sitting or a day or two) for a range of discipline-specific tasks, purposes, and audiences.*

"Write On" – page 159

Kindergarten-Grade 5
CCSS English Language Arts & Literacy: Writing Standards
- Kindergarten: *Production and distribution of Writing 5. With guidance and support from adults, respond to questions and suggestions from peers and add details to strengthen writing as needed.*
- Grade 1: *Production and distribution of Writing 5. With guidance and support from adults, focus on a topic, respond to questions and suggestions from peers, and add details to strengthen writing as needed.*
- Grade 2: *Production and distribution of Writing 5. With guidance and support from adults and peers, focus on a topic and strengthen writing as needed by revising and editing.*
- Grades 3 & 4: *Production and distribution of Writing 5. With guidance and support from peers and adults, develop and strengthen writing as needed by planning, revising, and editing.*
- Grade 5: *Production and distribution of Writing 5. With guidance and support from peers and adults, develop and strengthen writing as needed by planning, revising, editing, rewriting, or trying a new approach.*

CPSIA information can be obtained
at www.ICGtesting.com
Printed in the USA
LVHW020725170123
737163LV00001B/1

9 781792 425447